Wild CATALINA ISLAND

NATURAL SECRETS AND ECOLOGICAL TRIUMPHS

Frank J. Hein & Carlos de la Rosa

natural

HISTORY PRESS

Published by Natural History Press
A Division of The History Press
Charleston, SC 29403
www.historypress.net

First published 2013

ISBN 978-1-5402-2121-6

Library of Congress CIP data applied for.

Notice: The information in this book is true and complete to the best of our knowledge. It is offered without guarantee on the part of the authors or The History Press. The authors and The History Press disclaim all liability in connection with the use of this book.

For my wife, Terri, for her patience and understanding; for my friends for being kind and being there; to my mother, Audrey; and for my father, Bill, who reminded me when it mattered most that I was always meant to be a wildlife man.

—F.J. Hein

This book is dedicated to the next generation of Catalina residents and visitors, especially the younger crowd. May they fall in love with the island and take with them their desire to protect nature back to their homelands around the world. This is also dedicated to my wife, Claudia, and my children, Charlie and Lizzy, who share with me the wonders of discovery, science and conservation.

—C. de la Rosa

CONTENTS

ACKNOWLEDGEMENTS

Over the years, many, many people have been involved in creating the knowledge base that fed this book. It would be impossible to thank them all by name, but at the risk of an error of omission, we press on. First, a heartfelt thanks to all of the staff—past and present—at the Catalina Island Conservancy for being some of the best, brightest and hardest working teams we've had the joy of serving with. That is equally true for all of the good people—past and present—from the Institute for Wildlife Studies, whose contributions to the long-term survival of Catalina's wildlife cannot be overstated.

We would like to collectively thank the numerous researchers who have dedicated their lives to exploring, investigating and working out the natural order of things on Catalina, including its people, history, geology and biology. This book would not have been possible without their collective wisdom. We especially thank the following (in no particular order) for their special contributions: Wendy Teeter, Julie King, Calvin Duncan, Tony Summers, Charlie de la Rosa, Cindi Alvitre, Desiree Martinez, Steffani Jijón, Michael Herrera, Shane Barrow, Sarah Ratay, Denise Knapp, John Knapp, John Clark, Peter Dixon, Alexa Johnson, Aaron Morehouse, Bill Bushing, Deb Jensen, Jeff Jensen, Peter Schuyler, Dave Garcelon, Peter Sharpe, Robyn Powers, Darcee Guttilla, Frank Starkey, Rich Zanelli, Cliff Hague, Jeannine Pedersen, Stacey Otte, Lisa Stratton, Shaun Michael, Jeff Chapman, Douglas Comer, Michael Caterino, Thad Manuwal, Darren Sandquist, Scott Sillett, Rick Sweitzer, Angela Aarhus, Aaron Ramírez, Juliette Hart Finzy, Kristen

Andersen, Marla Daily, Steve Junak, Winston Vickers, Richard Denney, Shaun Evola, Roland de Govenain, Blanny Hagenah and so many more. And thank you, Leslie Baer, for, well, everything.

We would also like to thank the organizations that made images, materials and research available to us, including the Catalina Island Museum, the City of Avalon, the United States Geological Survey, the Santa Catalina Island Company and the Catalina Island Conservancy, where both authors worked and fell in love with the island.

Finally, a special thanks to the Catalina Island community for their undying love of the island and to the Wrigley and Offield families, who for generations have shared their love for Catalina, their time and resources, and their commitment to preserving and building upon the dream and the vision started so many years ago by William Wrigley Jr.

The images used in this book are from the collections of the authors or the Catalina Island Conservancy unless otherwise credited.

Preface
WHY THIS BOOK?

C atalina is a world-renowned adventure destination. It's a place where you can snorkel, dive, dine, kayak, hike, bike, walk and relax without ever leaving the city of Avalon. And for many, Avalon is all they ever see. If you look at a picture of Catalina from space, however, the first thing you'll notice is that Avalon occupies just a tiny speck of Catalina. As nice as Avalon is (and it is), there's more to Catalina—a whole lot more. If you've ever wondered what's beyond Avalon, this book is for you.

There's a lot to discover out here. There are plants and wildlife found only on Catalina and nowhere else on the planet. Catalina is by far the most accessible of all the Channel Islands and offers a wide variety of ways for visitors to access and experience its natural treasures. If you're not from around here, you're going to need a little help so you can get the most of your time. Whether you're on Catalina for a day, a weekend or are laying plans for a grand adventure on your return trip, this book can help you get the most out of your Catalina experience.

Catalina Island, while technically within the boundaries of Los Angeles County, is largely undeveloped, natural and wild. It is ecologically rare and isolated, yet it is just over an hour from Los Angeles by boat. Fragile yet durable, civilized but wild, it is all of these things and more. To help you understand Catalina, we'll take you on a journey from its unusual origins to its emergence from the ocean and its ecological birth and growth to the arrival of its first humans and, finally, to the modern day. Catalina is literally unique in the world, and the reasons why make a great story.

This book also explores the activities involved in managing the island's natural areas, including restoration of habitats, management of invasive species, monitoring for disease or newly arriving invasive species and more. We will also take a peek into the future of the island and how its fate is tied to the future of nature and our very planet. We'll talk about what makes Catalina so important for everyone who lives, works or plays there, and in the process, we will reveal why anyone who spends time here comes away feeling that Catalina is truly a special place.

This book grew from a series of lectures created by island naturalists designed to inform tour guides, educators, businesses and the community of Catalina about the ecological wonders of the place. The talks took participants on a journey from Catalina's birth through its human and natural history and showed how, against all odds, the island managed to not only survive human impacts but ultimately thrive ecologically and economically. The lectures became trainings, the trainings became stories and those stories became this book.

While written by scientists and informed by science, *Wild Catalina Island* is anything but a textbook. It's filled with inside stories, unusual facts and unforgettable imagery that come straight from the journals and lenses of the island's top ecological experts. They offer perspectives once known only to researchers and ecologists but now available to you.

Wild Catalina Island is a straightforward, compelling and fun read and the very best way to understand this amazing place before you arrive, while you are here or as you depart to plan your return adventure. Whether you are a first-time visitor or a lifelong lover of Catalina, this book will change the way you think about this jewel of the Pacific.

Read on, and prepare to see Catalina in a whole new light.

Frank and Carlos

Chapter 1

AN ISLAND IS BORN

The Catalina story begins much earlier than most stories you'll come across. It's a story that unfolds over millions of years, and things that happened millennia ago actually end up mattering quite a bit. With that in mind, let's start by looking at how Catalina Island came to be and how life in all its forms (humans included) got here, adapted and ultimately thrived.

The most logical place to start is around 30 million years ago. The forces that would create Catalina had been in play for many millions of years prior to this, but at around this time, things really started to come together. If, back then, you were to float above the California coastline looking for Catalina or any of the other Channel Islands, you wouldn't see them. The reason for that is that they hadn't come into existence yet. While you could certainly make out the general shape of North America, there would be a lot that would seem out of place. Where, for example, are Baja and the Sea of Cortez? Not born yet. You'd also see a calm blue ocean and a seemingly tranquil coastline, but your sense of tranquility would be wildly misplaced. The California coast then (as now) was a pressure cooker. Deep under the surface, collisions of a massive scale and force were taking place.

As you may know, the world's continents only seem stationary. They are, in fact, always in motion. Wherever you are right now, you're riding on a continental plate—a large sheet of earth's crust floating on a sea of magma pushing, pulling and colliding with other plates. In coastal California, we happen to be sitting at an intersection of plates that are engaged in a slow-

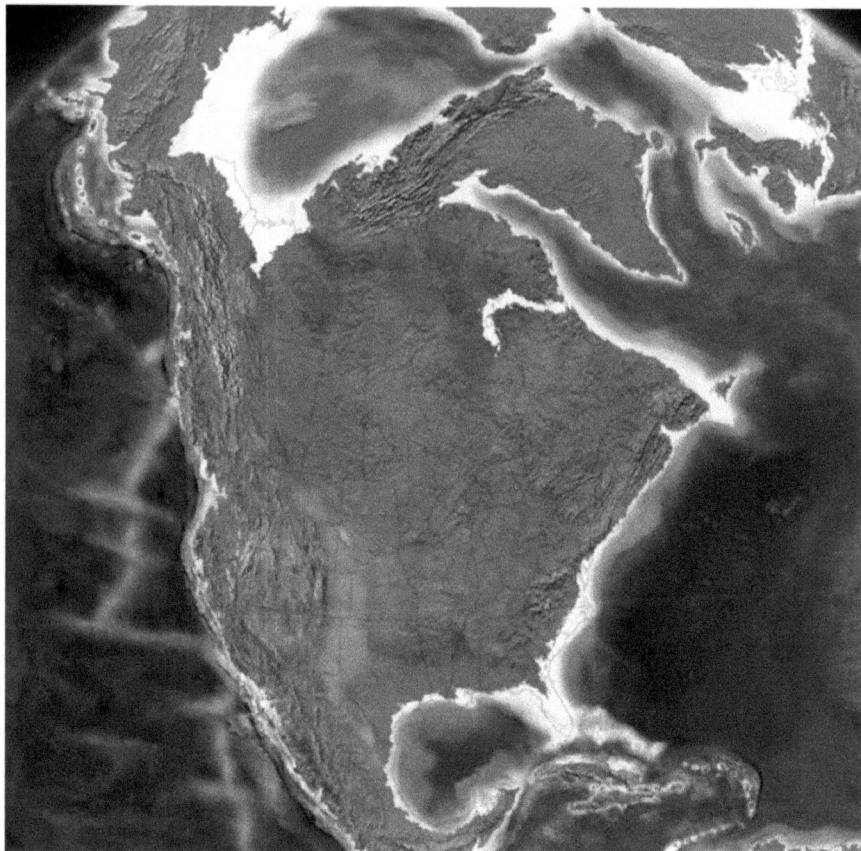

North America roughly 30 million years ago. Note the light fault lines in the Pacific Ocean showing the Farallon Plate on its way under as the Pacific Plate moves eastward. *Courtesy of United States Geological Survey.*

motion train wreck. As mellow as California may be socially, this place is geologically intense. When plates collide, the results can be monumental.

Another thing to know about continental plates is that they are big—really big. They can be thousands of miles long and many miles deep. The fact that they move slowly belies their incredible power. They create mountains and then move them. They tear continents apart. They are truly one of the great forces of nature. Hurricanes and tornados are tame by comparison. Even earthquakes, which are often caused by the movement and collision of the plates (what is known as plate tectonics), represent only a mere fraction of the power at play when the plates slip or jump along their edges.

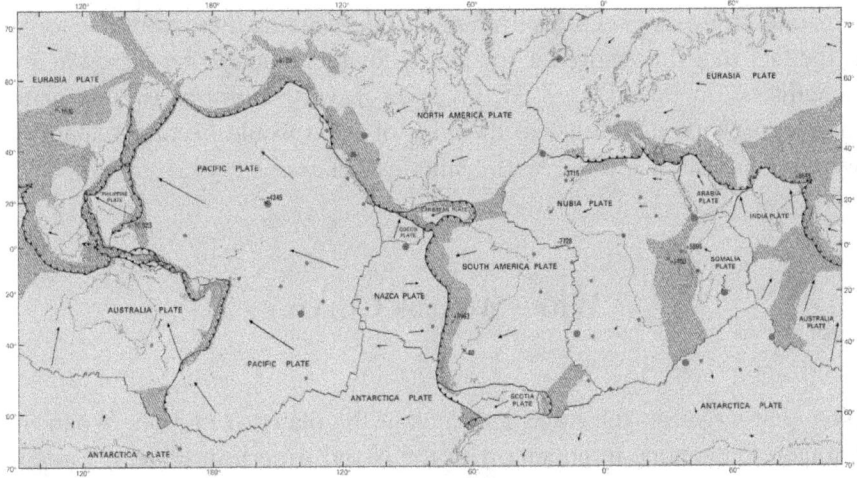

Depiction of the earth's continental plates. *Courtesy of This Dynamic Planet.*

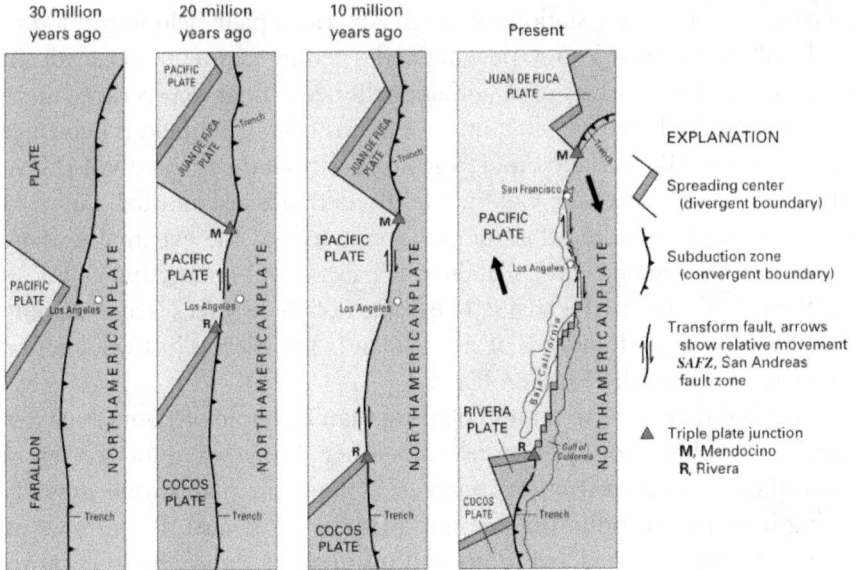

Detail showing the progression of the Farallon and Pacific Plate movements. *Courtesy of United States Geological Survey.*

The only thing that keeps us from really appreciating these awesome forces is the fact that they move far too slowly for the action to be seen. We are, nonetheless, at their mercy. At this point in earth's history, the big plates interacting with each other at the edge of what would become California were the Farallon and the North American Plates.

WHEN WORLDS COLLIDE

Now that we've set the stage, let's look at the plates in motion. When the Farallon Plate came in contact with the North American Plate, it came in low and heavy. Because of this, it "subducted" on impact (went under) and essentially just kept moving below the continent. It's still down there moving along deep under us. As we've mentioned, the underground forces where the two plates met were intense. Imagine the highest level of intensity you can, and then triple it. You'd probably still be underestimating the power of the collision. The relatively stationary North American plate held its ground as the Farallon slammed into it, pushing and grinding its way underneath. In the process, billions of tons of materials on the ocean floor were scraped away and left piled and scattered in a massive debris field. That field is known as the Continental Borderlands, and to geologists, this is the original Wild West. Geological features like the Continental Borderlands are unusual, and they are key to understanding the unique formation and the eventual ecology that would arise and become Catalina. It's also worth noting that collisions like these don't stop at the edges. The impact of these forces is also shaping the landscape many hundreds of miles inland. The Sierras just wouldn't be the Sierras without the Farallon Plate.

There's much more to plates colliding than a couple of continents just banging together and slipping past each other. There was a lot of friction down there, and with friction comes heat. Plus, the plates were actually diving into the semisolid magma and pushing it upward. Big pillows of magma called "plutons" were pushed up into the debris field, creating features that can still be found across all of the Channel Islands. The Northern Channel Islands, consisting of Anacapa, Santa Cruz, Santa Rosa and San Miguel, are all part of a single hunk of earth formed at this time called the Western Transverse Ranges Channel Islands Block. As large as these collective landmasses seem, they represent just a fraction

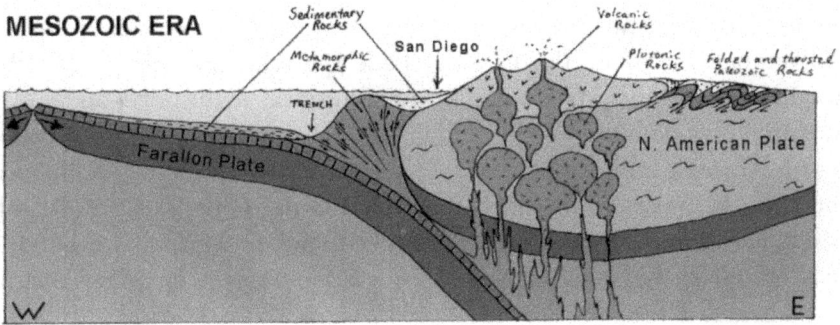

When plates collide! This close-up shows the forces that ultimately led to the formation of Catalina and the Channel Islands. *Courtesy of Gary Jacobson.*

Alone at sea, Catalina emerged as an oceanic island, waiting for life to arrive. Its proximity to Los Angeles County (seen here across the San Pedro Channel is Palos Verdes Peninsula) as well as its ecotourism infrastructure makes it the most visited of all the Channel Islands. *Courtesy of Frank Starkey.*

of the debris found in the Continental Borderlands. When the oceans are low—just as they were around 200 million years ago (the lowest level on record in the Permian-Triassic Period) or as little as twenty thousand years ago, when the levels were about 130 meters lower than today— Anacapa, Santa Cruz, Santa Rosa and San Miguel are revealed for what they really are: a single landmass called Santa Rosae. Things are different up there in spite of being shaped by the same forces as Catalina. Islands are like that—no two the same.

Eventually, most of the Farallon Plate split and dove down into the magma, leaving only small remnants grinding away to the north and south. Essentially, as time marched on, the main part of the Farallon slid under North America and out of the way. That massive debris field contained the building blocks from which Catalina and the other Channel Islands would rise. Eventually, sediments from the mainland also washed into the sea and piled up along the edge of the continent where the plates met. It was a beautiful mess.

As the Farallon continued its slide into the mantle, the Pacific Plate was hot on its heels. Without the Farallon Plate to hold it back, the Pacific Plate could now move more or less freely until it too slammed into North America. When this new contact occurred, things got really interesting. The Pacific Plate sat higher than the Farallon and didn't subduct under the North American Plate. Instead, the two plates pressed on each other, creaked and buckled until eventually something had to give. In time, the Pacific Plate began to slide north, taking a lot of the coast (and most of the Continental Borderlands) with it.

Twenty million years ago, before the Pacific Plate started moving north, the coastline was still more or less uniform—but that was about to change. Over the course of just a few million years, Baja and the Sea of Cortez were formed by literally being torn from the mainland by the Pacific Plate as it pulled it north. The entire edge of the continent from Mexico up to and beyond San Francisco started being pulled so hard it too began to shear away from the continent. The seam that runs along the North American Plate is known as the San Andreas Fault. One of the reasons scientists get so excited by the San Andreas Fault is that they know it's not a matter of if the edge of the continent is going to break more of North America free and shift north but when. It is moving a little bit every year, and sooner or later, it's really going to let loose. Nobody knows exactly what will happen, but when it does, one thing's for sure—it won't be subtle. Whoever said geology was boring didn't live in California. And if they did, they weren't paying attention.

Eventually, as pressures along the boundaries changed, the plates began to press upward and the Northern Channel Islands followed by the Southern Channel Islands began to emerge from the sea. It was at this time, a mere five million years ago, that Catalina was first thrust up and out of the ocean, and an island was born. While it's true that the substrate that makes up

Catalina is made up of material that's hundreds of millions of years old, an island isn't an island until it emerges from the water. That makes Catalina's "born-on date" five million years ago.

When Catalina first saw the light of day, the island was located down south near Baja California, but it's been moving north ever since. On average, Catalina continues to race northward at somewhere between three and seven millimeters per month. That's about the same speed your fingernails grow, and it's pretty fast. Just for fun, choose a fingernail and don't cut it for a few weeks and you'll see what we mean.

CONTINENTAL VS. OCEANIC ISLANDS: WHAT'S THE DIFFERENCE?

When Catalina was new to the world, it would have seemed empty, raw and devoid of life; it had a clean slate. Sure, bacteria and the odd shoreline plant or bug and other scatterings of life would be present, but to most of us, it would appear barren and lifeless. This is how an oceanic island starts life—naked and alone, waiting for life to arrive.

But not all islands come into the world this way. On the other end of the spectrum are continental islands, which are closely associated with the mainland and therefore start off with a goodly complement of life. Continental islands begin life with their ecology already in place and then break away from the mainland, ecology intact, and move out to sea. Eventually, if the island becomes isolated from the mainland, the evolution of the ecology it had when it departed will begin to diverge. The key is that continental islands evolve from a point of ecological richness borrowed from the original landmass. These kinds of islands get to start life with their very own ecological starter kit and then diverge from the mainland over time. Catalina didn't have it so easy.

Catalina is classified as an oceanic island because it was born at sea. In its entire life as an island, it's never been attached or even close to the mainland. This may seem like a fine point, but for Catalina it makes all the difference in the world. Catalina would have to begin from scratch. How did Catalina go from almost nothing to the rich, ecologically significant island we know and love today? We'll tackle all of this and more in the next chapter, but before we go, a word about uniqueness. Wholly new ecological systems don't come around every day, and Catalina Island is different from all other islands in ways that matter.

It isn't just that a new ecological system came to be but also when and where it came on the scene. Catalina's emergence off the coast of North America five million years ago was a once-in-a-planet event. It hadn't happened before, and it's not going to happen the same way ever again. When we talk about Catalina being unique, we mean it in the truest sense of the word. And because of this uniqueness, there are things about Catalina that evolved differently than any other place in the world. How could it be otherwise? It's interesting that people tend to pick up on this fact even if they don't know anything about the ecology of the island. You can kind of sense it; it's different here.

Now, to become the Catalina we know today, the island had to emerge at a certain time, in a certain place, with a certain set of soils and a proximity to a certain set of natural resources. On top of that, those bits of nature—snails, spiders, squirrels, quail, grasses, oaks, etc.—we now see as "normal" had to be able to get here somehow. Catalina is defined as much by which species made it here as by which didn't. And which species got there first would've mattered too. For example, if you managed to find your way across twenty-three miles of open ocean and were the first and only squirrel species on the island, you'd get to occupy every possible squirrel niche. If you were the second squirrel species to arrive (long after the first), you'd find a squirrel army already entrenched and ready to reduce your odds of making it. Species diversity and sequencing was important for plants, bugs and birds too, and as you'll see, it made a big difference in how things turned out.

As we enter the brave new world of Catalina Island's ecology, marvel with us at the series of very unlikely events that had to happen precisely as they did to create this extraordinary ecological jewel of the Pacific.

Chapter 2
COMING OF AGE

In the previous chapter, we left Catalina new, barren, rocky and isolated—a landscape waiting for life. In terms of terrestrial ecology, that's essentially how it was. Catalina's isolation and emergence far out at sea pretty much assured a blank slate scenario in the uplands, but for Catalina's coastline, it was another story entirely.

Catalina's coasts would have been teeming with life as soon as they came into existence. Much as we see today, kelp forests would have grown; fish would have sought out new habitats; and seals, otters, sea lions, marlin, grouper, dolphins, abalone, crabs, kelp, bladder pods and more would have ringed the island almost as soon as the shoreline came into existence. The reason for this seemingly paradoxical scenario is that for oceanic life, oceans simply aren't barriers. It's easy to see how a dolphin could get to Catalina. Kelp? A cakewalk. In terms of aquatic ecologies, Catalina was directly connected to the whole wide ocean, but for species like oaks, flowers, mosses and mice, the oceans presented a very real and challenging barrier.

Before we head upland, take a moment to imagine the contrast between Catalina's thriving, connected marine and near-shore environments and the freshly emerged, ecologically thin and isolated character of the rest of the island. We've hinted at this already, but the reason the shoreline environment thrived while the rest of the island waited in quiet desperation for life to arrive is isolation. Isolation changes everything. How Catalina's lands evolved from barren rock into the rich and beautiful ecological landscapes we see today is a fascinating story, and it will take a bit of unpacking.

For kelp, the ocean is no barrier at all. Note the round bladders, perfectly suited for floating on the tides. *Courtesy of Carlos de la Rosa.*

Just add dirt! The gradual formation of soils on Catalina was a prerequisite for the survival of most terrestrial life forms to come. *Courtesy of Catalina Island Conservancy.*

While it's tempting to jump right in and imagine how a squirrel or a lizard could possibly have ever made its way to Catalina, there's not much point to it yet, and for one very good reason. It doesn't matter if you beat the odds and make it to Catalina if you can't survive without food or shelter—and food and shelter can't generally get started without soil. Soil would have been in very short supply in Catalina's early existence, and without soil, terrestrial species would have been more or less doomed.

What is soil anyway? We mostly know it as the stuff in which plants grow, the material one buys in bags at the gardening supply store or the surface that we plow through and turn over to prepare for planting. Soil is precious and renewable but also easily lost. Soil can take centuries to build and can be washed away forever in a single massive flood. Soil is the matrix that sustains life. But at the very beginning, soil starts with little bits of dust. Dust collected from the surface of dry ground is light, made of tiny particles, able to travel great distances carried by the wind and able to settle into crevices and fill in tiny gaps between hard rocks. But this tiny pile of fine powdery stuff has an interesting characteristic—it can trap moisture and hold it. In a climate where rainfall is highly seasonal and in short supply, that's a pretty handy attribute.

Dust provides substrate and mineral nutrients, while water provides the essential element for life to thrive. Together, they become soil, and with it, seedlings can take root and growth can occur. As things grow and eventually die, their organic matter is added to the soil, making it richer. Once this essential cycle begins, it is largely self-perpetuating—a perfect process that quite literally manufactures the foundation for more complex life.

The other thing about soil is that it's not evenly distributed. Catalina's steep terrain tends to create conditions for soil to constantly move downhill into arroyos and other low-lying areas. But for our purposes, it's enough that soil would eventually form at a quantity and quality that seeds of all kinds could germinate and take hold. This is one of the first of many steps needed for Catalina to develop a fully functioning ecology. While it's true there weren't any humans around to see it happen, it's likely that soil formation on Catalina went something like this: As the island emerged, it was also being eroded. Wind, rain, heat and cold all conspired to whittle away any exposed landmass. If not for the fact that Catalina was rising faster than it was being worn away, there wouldn't be a Catalina to talk about. Lucky for us, the island is still emerging faster than it's being worn down. In any event, these forces slowly turned boulders into rocks, rocks into stones and stones to dust. Gravity ensured that as materials broke apart they migrated downward into ravines and low-lying areas, where they collected into concentrated areas of something we'd call soil.

Catalina's early soils wouldn't have been terribly nutrient rich, but luckily not all plants need rich soil. In fact, lots of plants thrive on nutrient-poor soils. The key here is that soil of some kind began to form and lay out something of an ecological welcome mat for seeds to take hold. And all it would have taken would be for just a few species to arrive and thrive to start the cycle of life and death. In time, decaying plant matter would gradually add organic matter to the dust and gravel and perpetuate a slow accumulation of nutrients across the island. This would have created variations of soil richness across the island as well since varying topographies would have influenced the location of soils differently. All of this would have resulted in a variety of scenarios for seeds to take hold, establish and thrive.

With each successive season, plants would have grown and died, dropping their organic matter just a few inches from their roots. Year by year, inch by inch and acre by acre, organic matter would have marched across the island. With apologies to soil scientists and master gardeners, we'll move on from here, lest we descend into a treatise on the technical aspects of soil formation and nutrient cycling. The point is that plants couldn't make it on Catalina until soil had been formed, and bugs, snails, lizards and mice couldn't make it until plants and the food, shelter and diversity they provided were on the ground. And so, with soil at our feet, let's welcome terrestrial life to Catalina.

Today, Catalina has a significant (and quite lovely) functioning ecology, complete with hundreds and hundreds of species. But if the place is so isolated, how did all that life get there? That is the million-dollar question, and it has a million-dollar answer. While we did say that Catalina is isolated, we never said it was *completely* isolated. It's clearly against the odds for cacti, oaks, rodents, plants and snakes to get here, but clearly it wasn't impossible. Almost anything can happen if there's enough time. Catalina has had just over five million years to beat the odds, and it needed pretty much all of it.

Five millions years. Let's get our heads around that. Humans have a really hard time thinking in terms of millions of years. One reason is that (with a little luck) we only live to be around eighty to one hundred years old. And as a result, we consider the likelihood of things happening based on a roughly one-hundred-year framework. When we think about the odds of getting struck by lightning, what we're really imagining is the odds of getting struck by lightning in our lifetime. According to the National Weather Service, your odds of being struck by lightning during an eighty-year lifespan are about one in ten thousand. That's rare enough that if it's happened to you, it makes for a pretty remarkable story, and one worth telling. But imagine that you had an eight-hundred-year lifespan. Your chances of getting struck just moved to one in one thousand. If you lived to be eight thousand? One in one hundred. If you lived eighty thousand years, one in every ten people you meet would have been struck by lightning, and the event would hardly be worth mentioning. We'd all know several people who'd been struck. The take-home point is that time changes all odds. It just does.

Now just imagine how many other unlikely events would become commonplace if you lived to be 800,000 years old. Your chances of seeing a tornado, surviving a car crash or finding a diamond lying on the ground would change from very unlikely to likely. Now imagine living to be a million years or five million years old and you'll be in the right frame of mind to contemplate the pacing of the arrival and evolution of life on Catalina. Let's get started.

There are three main ways that life arrives on Catalina, and we call them the three *W*s: Wing, Wind and Wave. They're all pretty straightforward. Wing, as the name implies, refers to things flying here. You can easily imagine a bird such as a gull or an eagle setting its sights on a distant island and heading across the water toward it. But many things other than birds also arrive on Catalina by wing. A seed stuck in the feathers of an osprey, for example, falls to the ground as the bird arrives and preens. Or a songbird feeding on berries on the mainland arrives and poops out a batch of seeds in their own handy fertilizer packet, ready to grow. Even some strong insect fliers, like dragonflies or moths, can negotiate the distance and arrive laden with eggs to start a new generation. Again, given enough time, all of these scenarios are bound to happen. But flying even twenty-three miles across open water isn't quite as easy as it seems. Most big birds rely on thermals to provide lift as they go, and oceans don't generate much in the way of thermals. That means powered flight all the way, and birds die every year trying to make the crossing. Turkey vultures, for example, rely almost exclusively on thermals for long-distance flight, and while they're common on the mainland, they're strangely absent on Catalina. Species other than birds can also fly, like bats for example, and we do have those. They would have needed time and a little luck to make the trip, but they and whatever they happened to be hitchhiking on or in them made it too.

Our next *W* is wind. Anyone who's ever blown on a dandelion and watched those white tufts take to the sky knows that some seeds are ideally suited for wind distribution. Seeds, pollen and even bugs are constantly drifting in the air and falling from the sky. Everywhere you go, it's raining DNA. Some of

Above: Arrival by wave. Mats of vegetation, usually created after large storms, can be an excellent vehicle for species to make the journey to our remote island. *Courtesy of Frank J. Hein.*

Opposite, top: Birds arrived by wing, but other things often came along for the ride. Seeds can cling to feathers or be eaten and eventually dropped onto the ground in their own little fertilizer packets. *Courtesy of Catalina Island Conservancy.*

Opposite, bottom: Arrival by wind. Seeds aren't the only things that can fly in via the breeze. Billions of insects are also carried by the wind, constantly moving over our heads. Some of those bugs were destined to fall onto Catalina. *Courtesy of Carlos de la Rosa.*

this life makes its way into higher air columns and even into the jet stream, where it can travel remarkable distances. There are billions and trillions of bugs and seeds hovering above us and randomly falling from the sky on any given day. However, most of these bits of life don't have any control over where they're going to land. Catalina is just a tiny speck in the sea, but sooner or later, a seed, a bug or a spore is bound to land here.

Our last *W* is wave, and it's our lowest-odds travel plan. A typical scenario would go like this. Millions of years ago, in a canyon in what would someday be known as Los Angeles, a winter storm with heavy rains causes a major flash flood. Waters rise, and trees, stumps and mats of tangled vegetation are washed out to sea. Looking closely, we see bugs, small mammals, seeds and even saplings intertwined and floating out to sea toward Catalina. At least they *might* be floating toward Catalina. They might also be drifting out to sea to perish. There's a lot of ocean and not much island out here, so the odds of making it are pretty slim. And there's also the not-so-small matter of staying alive long enough to survive the journey. Most things carried by waves or ocean currents drift past Catalina or die at sea—most, but not all. Sooner or later, a raft full of life is going to drift into a sheltered island bay and disgorge its cargo of creatures. With all of these mechanisms at play and with millions of years to narrow the odds, you can see that the arrival of some sort of life on Catalina is almost a foregone conclusion. Things were bound to get here, and sure enough, that's exactly what happened. But getting to Catalina, it turns out, would be the easy part.

Chapter 3
SURVIVOR!

Let the Competition Begin

Life on an Island: It's Different Here...

Any visitor arriving by boat to Catalina Island notices almost immediately that life on this sleepy little island is different. From a human perspective, you notice that there are very few cars in the town and that most people have adapted to a different lifestyle. They've adapted to walking, riding bikes and getting around in golf carts. Imagine that. You notice there are no traffic lights and only a few stop signs. You observe other things missing as well, like fast-food restaurants and big superstores. Catalina doesn't have those. The people of Catalina adapt their shopping habits to get by without them. Catalina Islanders have access to stores, but fewer of them. They have restaurants, but not many, and they have a grocer, but just one. That tends to limit one's choices. For people, the main difference between Catalina and the mainland is that we have fewer options—less diversity of just about everything. But in spite of this, Catalina Islanders have a pretty good quality of life. As long as the one grocer keeps stocking food, we can all eat. As long as our one electronics store is here, we can get our technology fix.

We point this out because Catalina's ecology has the same issues at play, and they dramatically influence the character of the natural systems here. Only certain species make it to Catalina, and the ones that do make it find themselves getting by on less than they're used to and dealing with situations that are different from those they would find on their original mainland

Above: Shooting stars cover Catalina's hillsides for a brief and shining moment each spring. *Courtesy of Frank J. Hein.*

Opposite: Hotels, shops and restaurants line Front Street in Avalon, a city ready to accommodate the nearly one million visitors to Catalina each year. *Courtesy of Frank J. Hein.*

homes. For example, there are many species of fox on the mainland whereas Catalina has just one. We have only one species of squirrel here, while there are dozens and dozens on the mainland. From an ecologist's perspective, there's less biological diversity here, and that makes our ecology more fragile. Biodiversity, after all, is essentially the total number of distinct biological organisms found in an area. It's like a house of cards, but the Catalina house is built from a much smaller deck. The foundation and ecological stability is a little shakier and a lot more vulnerable to outside forces. While Catalina's ecology is fragile, it doesn't mean it's always teetering on the brink. It just means that with fewer moving parts, each part becomes more critical to the functionality of the whole system. As a result, it becomes incredibly important to protect every card in the deck, or in this case, every species of plant and animal on the island.

We're starting to get closer to understanding what makes Catalina so unique, but we're not done setting the stage just yet. It's not just that we have fewer species getting by on less, it's also that many of the species we have can't be found anywhere else. They've changed as a result of being isolated for millions of years. So Catalina is not just ecologically fragile, its ability to function relies on species and subspecies that you couldn't bring in from somewhere else if you lost them.

ISOLATION BREEDS A DIFFERENT KIND OF ANIMAL...AND RATHER QUICKLY

We've already explored the ways things get to the island, and we've shown how the island's isolation is a major barrier for the types and species that can settle here. Some things can get here; most things can't. Some beat great odds to get here, but getting here is just the first step. The thing is, once you get to Catalina, you have to find a way to survive. That generally means getting by on different foods or a smaller variety of what you're used to. You need to adapt your behavior and diet right away or perish. Insisting on eating seeds that you're used to but that don't exist here is not a long-term survival strategy. So you adjust. You adapt. If all goes well, you survive to pass on your genes. Assuming you can find a mate that is, and the odds of that are ridiculously low. If there are others of your species on the island, there won't be many. Your choice of mates is going to be severely limited.

And this is where things start to get interesting in a hurry. If you arrived on Catalina as say, a pregnant squirrel, and managed to get your litter to survive, your young might not have any other squirrels to mate with. That doesn't mean you wouldn't have any potential mates. It's just that they'd be your immediate family. New blood (literally) doesn't get to Catalina on a regular basis, and there are only so many genes to go around. The odds that you'll be breeding with a close relative go way up. That means that if you have a genetic predisposition for, let's say, long legs, there are higher odds that your cousin or sister will have those genes too. If long legs are favored in your family line, and if having longer legs isn't some sort of fatal attribute, longer legs are likely to be seen in the population at a greater rate than on the mainland. That's just a random example, and as far as we know, Catalina's ground squirrels have more or less standard-sized legs. They did, however, become much larger—more on that later. For now, the point is that a limited and isolated gene pool will lead to skewed outcomes when compared to a gene pool that's not isolated. It's one of the reasons that island species quickly diverge from their mainland counterparts.

The Catalina California ground squirrel, a giant among squirrels and an island icon. *Courtesy of Carlos de la Rosa.*

Without a regular exchange of "fresh" genes, the same old genes will get over-represented through inbreeding, and our squirrel species will continue changing until they become so different that they become an entirely new species or, perhaps, a subspecies, which is exactly what happened with Catalina's squirrels. Exactly how and why a species changes over time is worth a closer look.

Just remember, time plays a big role in all of this. It takes many thousands of years and thousands of generations for new species to evolve, and as we've seen, who got here first, the conditions they found when they got here and the makeup of their DNA all play a role in their evolution. Just about every species on the island was influenced by the forces of island isolation.

THE FOUNDER EFFECT

When a few individuals of a mainland population arrive on an island and successfully settle there (meaning, they start to reproduce and create their own new population) they bring with them only a small portion of the genetic makeup of the main population. This means that a lot of the full genetic potential of the species—the variability accumulated through thousands of years of breeding, growing, adapting and mutations—is largely lost in favor of the sample of genes represented in these few "founders." This new population can result in something very different than the original source group in relatively few generations.

Founder effects are a key feature of island speciation, that is, the formation of new or modified species from an original parent population or species. A key element of this process is isolation. If new individuals from the parent population continue to arrive, bringing fresh genes with them, the island population probably won't change much from the original species. You see this on Catalina all the time. New breeding eagles may arrive from the mainland with relative frequency, and as a result, the individuals found on the island remain a genetic match with those found on the mainland.

So species adapted, changed and became different (or stayed the same) as a result of gene-flow rates and the unique selective pressures of predation, competition and environmental challenges they faced. The net result? Catalina is now home to over sixty species or subspecies that exist here and nowhere else in the world. As research continues, it's almost certain that number will rise.

They're back! After decades of effort, our nation's symbol once again thrives on Catalina and the other Channel Islands. *Courtesy of Carlos de la Rosa.*

So with soil on the ground, plants thriving on the soil and insects, mice, squirrels and more thriving, we find ourselves at the cusp of the island's coming-of-age ecology. There have been millions of years of arrivals, settlers and founders with innumerable failures (most of which we'll never know about) but also a few notable successes, which have culminated into the wonderful ecosystem of Catalina. Catalina Island is host to hundreds of species of plants, mammals, amphibians, reptiles, birds, insects and other invertebrates, not to mention lichens and mosses, fungi and bacteria that also have, against steep odds, established themselves on Catalina. While not as rich in species as the mainland, Catalina Island has, in its own way, become rich in habitats and the species they support. In the next chapter, we'll take you on a journey in which we'll discover dwarves and giants, hotspots and the evolutionary stars that make Catalina the ecological wonder that it is.

Chapter 4
THE ECOLOGY OF CATALINA ISLAND

Uniqueness Abounds

Of Giants and Dwarves: Strange but True Stories from Catalina's Wildlands

One fascinating thing that happens on islands is the change that can occur in body size of certain species. Driven by a scarcity (or unusual bounty) of food resources, different physical challenges posed by the new environment, changes in genetic makeup from limited gene flow and perhaps a combination of all these factors, certain island species tend to get smaller or larger than their mainland counterparts. This happens often enough that scientists found it necessary to come up with names for these phenomena: "island gigantism" and "island dwarfism." This may be hard to believe, but Catalina is home to real giants, and we have real dwarfs too.

Our giants include the Catalina California ground squirrel (*Spermophilus beecheyi nesioticus*), the Catalina Island quail (*Callipepla californica catalinensis*) and the Saint Catherine's lace (*Eriogonum giganteum var. giganteum*). Among our dwarfs, we have the dwarf flax (*Hesperolinon micranthum*) and the dwarf sack clover (*Trifolium depauperatum*). Perhaps our most famous island dwarf is the Catalina Island fox (*Urocyon littoralis catalinae*).

The Catalina Island fox is a descendant of the mainland gray fox, which is significantly larger. That means that the time foxes spent on Catalina exerted pressures that favored smallness. Why did they get smaller when other things got bigger? Well, for one thing, small islands tend to create limits for big animals. If you're used to roaming large areas of land in order to make a living and are suddenly constrained to a small chunk of rock out in the ocean with little room to roam, being huge would present some problems. Not only might you not be able to find enough to eat, but you could also easily eat yourself out of house and home. Being a little smaller would have its advantages. And since there are literally no other mammalian predators on the island, it wouldn't matter if you couldn't hold your own against a red fox, a badger or a mountain lion.

It also turns out that with different and almost certainly limited prey options available, Catalina's foxes had to adapt to a new diet. A really nice study conducted by the State of California's Department of Fish and Game across all of the Channel Islands showed that Catalina's foxes are more vegetarian in diet than any other island fox. Would a smaller body size make it easier to forage through tight brush? Might smaller paws increase their capacity to get at fruits or seeds? Might the lower nutrient value of a more vegetarian diet favor a smaller body? Those are good theories, and there are a few dozen others that might account for their dwarfism. But whatever the exact reasons, the realities of Catalina favored a smaller fox—so much so that Catalina Island foxes are now small enough that they can sometimes be mistaken for housecats.

While the precise interplay of genetics, habitat availability, diet and competition aren't completely understood for every species, we can say the following with some certainty: Over time, wild things will find their

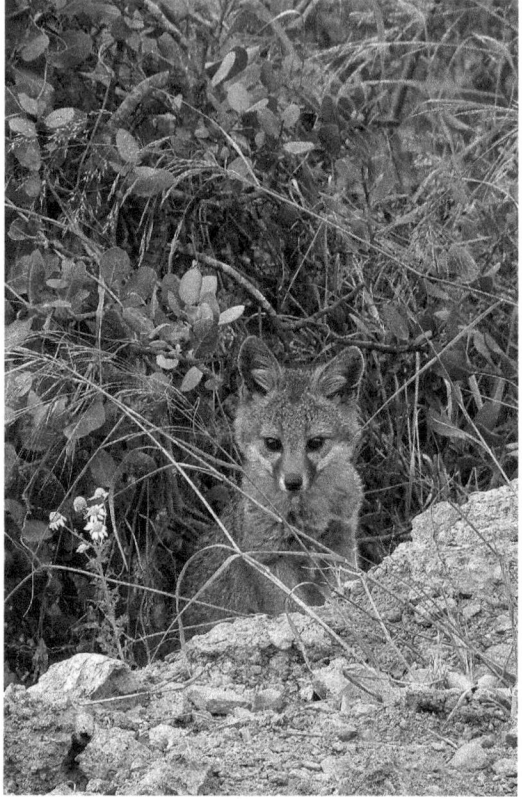

Nearly lost but now returned, the Catalina Island fox stands as a warning of the delicate nature of species on islands and, thankfully, as an endangered species success story! *Courtesy of Carlos de la Rosa.*

St. Catherine's lace is a Catalina Island endemic as well as an island giant. *Courtesy of Carlos de la Rosa.*

equilibrium with their environment, and as a rule of thumb, if you're very large when you get to a small island, there are reasonably good odds that you'll trend smaller over time. If you're tiny when you get here (and there are lots of open niches), the odds are that you'll trend a little larger over time. It's worth noting that often a species arrives and stays the same size it always was, with its equilibrium on Catalina apparently matching that of its original locale. Be sure to look for some of our giants and dwarfs when you journey to Catalina, and don't miss the chance to tell your friends back home that you honestly saw a giant!

MEDITERRANEAN-TYPE CLIMATE AND CATALINA

You may have already heard that Catalina (and most of coastal California) is located in a Mediterranean-type climate. This name comes from the

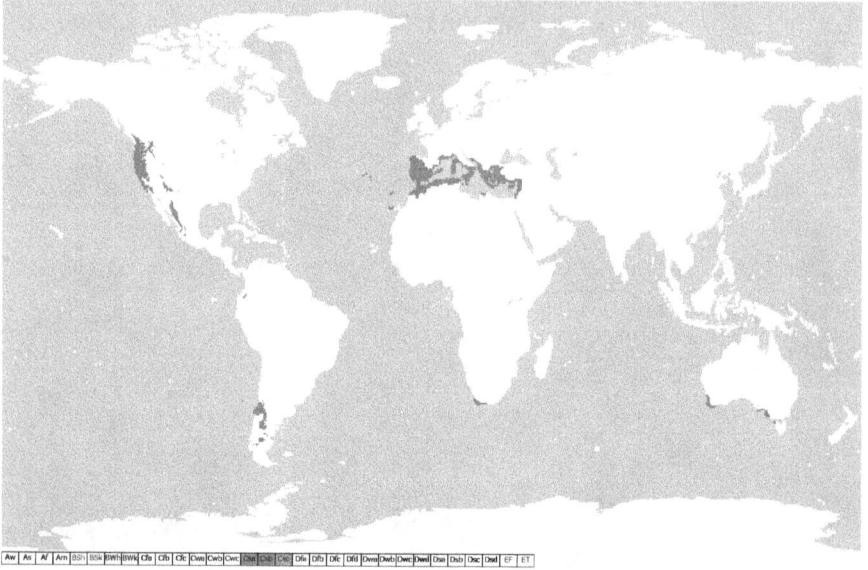

This map shows Mediterranean-type habitats around the world. *PD-US.*

true Mediterranean region, which spans most of southern Europe and northern Africa, including Italy, Spain, Portugal, Greece, Turkey, Egypt, Morocco, Algeria and many other countries. What's so special about the Mediterranean? It never gets too hot, and it never gets too cold. It's also fairly dry, averaging just ten to twenty inches of rain per year, and is in close proximity to the ocean. All of these characteristics make for a pretty cushy place for people to live and is one of the big reasons that people flock to these kinds of climates.

There are seven regions in the world that share a similar Mediterranean-type climate: the Mediterranean itself, parts of central coastal Chile, southwestern South Africa, parts of western and southern Australia, sections of central Asia and Southern California, where Catalina is located. And while the plants and animals are different in each region, they also share similar characteristics, like tolerance for dry periods, warm-to-hot dry summers, mild to cool winters, plant adaptations to deal with infrequent fire and lots of endemic species.

Mediterranean-type climates are one of the most endangered habitats in the world, mostly because they are relatively small in total area and they have been hugely modified and impacted by people. In recent years,

Catalina has become something of an exception in that the largest portion of the island is under conservation and protection and the negative effects of many human activities have been controlled or are in the process of being reversed. This is yet another reason that Catalina is important on a global scale.

How Is the Nature of Catalina Organized? In Habitats

People are usually pretty good at recognizing where they are. In general terms, even a child would easily know whether he or she was standing in a city, suburb or on a farm. There are obvious cues that tell us that. Tall buildings, busy streets and lots of cars? City. Nice houses with mowed yards and few cars? Suburbs. Wide fields of corn, barns and silos? Farm. Similarly, most of us can tell a forest from a pasture or wetlands. We generally refer to these broad categories as "habitats."

Animals' lives depend on their capacity to recognize and respond to the characteristics of various habitats. They also prefer certain habitats to others. Acorn woodpeckers, for example, don't go too far from oak trees because that's where they can find acorns! Tadpoles are obligated to stay in their aquatic habitat, and osprey, as fishermen, stick close to the water.

Habitats are determined by certain features such as terrain, microclimate (moisture and temperature), exposure to the sun and closeness to the ocean. Basic sets of features allow us to organize the landscape into fairly distinct habitats or ecological zones. On Catalina, we recognize chaparral, coastal sage scrub, woodlands, sand dunes, oak forest, pastures or grasslands, lakes, streams and their riparian (streamside) forests. We also have urban areas like Avalon and Two Harbors, of course.

Let's briefly explore some of these Catalina habitats and discover what makes them so distinct and unique. As you might expect, even though these categories are also found on the mainland, their Catalina counterparts are somewhat different. So, the island chaparral on Catalina is similar but not quite the same as the mainland California chaparral. Why? For all the usual reasons of isolation, limited gene flow, founder effects and more. The same forces impact almost every aspect of island life.

Island Chaparral

The island chaparral found on Catalina is characterized by dense thickets of shrubs and dwarf trees. The plants tend to have hard leaves that, when accumulating on the soil, release resins and waxes, making the substrate unfriendly to other plants and highly flammable. Fire plays an important role in chaparral, and many species have developed adaptations to recover quickly from fires. On the island, the chaparral tends to be sparser than on the mainland, giving the habitat the look of a dwarf forest. Some of the common species found in the island chaparral are the island scrub oak (*Quercus pacifica*), lemonade berry (*Rhus integrifolia*), toyon (*Heteromeles arbutifolia*), island redberry (*Rhamnus pirifolia*), ceanothus (*Ceanothus spp.*), chamise (*Adenostoma fasciculatum*), Catalina manzanita (*Arctostaphylos catalinae*), the endemic Catalina mahogany (*Cercocarpus traskiae*) and island mountain mahogany (*Cercocarpus betuloides var. blancheae*).

These small little amphora-like flowers bloom on the Catalina manzanita, a species endemic to the island and representative of the chaparral habitat. *Courtesy of Carlos de la Rosa.*

Island Woodland

This habitat is characterized by the presence of three very unique species: the Catalina ironwood (*Lyonothamnus floribundus ssp. floribundus*, a Catalina endemic), the beautiful island oak (*Quercus tomentella*, an island endemic also found on other Channel Islands) and Catalina cherry (*Prunus ilicifolia lyonii*). Most of the species mentioned under chaparral are also found in the island woodlands, along with grasses and herbaceous species and ferns. There are also some forests made up of non-native or introduced species. The pine forests of blackjack and the eucalyptus stands lining Summit Road are good examples of this. Typical species of animals found in chaparral and island woodland habitats include the Catalina ground squirrel (*Spermophilus beecheyi nesioticus*), the Bewick's Wren (*Thryomanes bewickii catalinae*) and the Hutton's Vireo (*Vireo huttoni unitti*), as well as the ubiquitous Catalina Island fox.

Island oaks often form small dwarf-like forest patches. *Courtesy of Carlos de la Rosa.*

Coastal Sage Scrub

Although well represented on Catalina, this is one of the most threatened habitats in California due to its conversion to development. The coastal sage scrub on the island is dominated by low shrubs (two meters in height or less) that tend to be drought tolerant. The name comes from the presence of several very fragrant species collectively called "sages" such as the California sagebrush (*Artemisia californica*), white sage (*Salvia apiana*) and black sage (*Salvia mellifera*). Other common species include the tart-fruited lemonade berry (*Rhus integrifolia*), the bush sunflower (*Encelia californica*), St. Catherine's lace (*Eriogonum giganteum var. giganteum*), bedstraw (*Galium spp.*), silver clover (*Lotus argophyllus var. argenteus*), island deerweed (*Lotus dendroideus*), red bush monkeyflower (*Mimulus aurantiacus*) and laurel sumac (*Malosma laurina*). Endemics to Catalina Island include the St. Catherine's lace (another island giant) mentioned above, the Catalina bedstraw (*Galium catalinense catalinense*) and the Catalina yerba santa (*Eriodictyon traskiae traskiae*). Most of these species produce beautiful flowers in the spring, which is a great time to explore the interior of the island. Another

White sage is one of the more aromatic of the coastal sage plants and can be smelled from many yards away when it's in full fragrance. *Courtesy of Rich Zanelli.*

species commonly found in this habitat is the coastal prickly pear cactus (*Opuntia littoralis*), which is not usually found in mainland sage scrub habitats. Typical animals of the sage scrub include the Catalina Southern Pacific rattlesnake (*Crotalus oreganus helleri*, a possible new endemic subspecies for the island) and the beautiful Island loggerhead shrike (*Lanius ludovicianus anthonyi*), also found on Santa Rosa and Santa Cruz Islands.

Maritime Cactus Scrub

A type of coastal sage scrub, this habitat is dominated by several unique cactus species that form dense stands on some hillsides on the ocean side of the island. Typical species include the velvet cactus (*Bergerocactus emoryi*), coastal cholla (*Opuntia prolifera*), coastal prickly pear (*Opuntia littoralis*, an important food source for many animals, including the Catalina Island fox), California boxthorn (*Lycium californicum*), California sagebrush (*Artemisia californica*), bush sunflower (*Encelia californica*), the rare and unique cliff spurge (*Euphorbia misera*) and lemonade berry, as well as herbaceous species such as coast weed (*Amblyopappus pusillus*), aphanisma (*Aphanisma blitoides*), coast goldenbush (*Isocoma menziesii*), the beautiful and rare Emory's rockdaisy (*Perityle emoryi*), saltbush (*Atriplex spp.*), several species of liveforever (*Dudleya spp.*) and wishbone bush (*Mirabilis californica*).

The prickly pear is typical of the maritime cactus scrub. Its fruits are an important food source for birds and foxes. *Courtesy of Carlos de la Rosa.*

Coastal Bluff Scrub

Found in very specific sites along the coast on ocean bluffs, this habitat is characterized by dwarf shrubs, herbaceous plants and a number of not-too-tall woody species. This habitat presents very harsh conditions for plant growth, with high winds, salt spray and very dry soils. Because of its inaccessibility, many rare and endemic plants have found refuge here from introduced browsers and grazers. Common species in the coastal bluffs include the spectacular giant coreopsis (*Coreopsis gigantea*), Catalina crossosoma (*Crossosoma californicum*), several species of liveforever (*Dudleya spp.*), St. Catherine's lace (*Eriogonum giganteum var. giganteum*), island buckwheat (*E. grande var. grande*), wooly sunflower (*Eriophyllum nevinii*), island tarplant (*Hemizonia clementina*) and Lyon's phacelia (*Phacelia lyonii*).

The liveforever's beautiful flowers adorn the rocky surfaces of the coastal bluffs. *Courtesy of Carlos de la Rosa.*

This salina habitat is located at Little Harbor on Catalina. Palms were introduced during the movie-making heydays. *Courtesy of Carlos de la Rosa.*

Coastal Marsh

Definitely a rare habitat on the island, the coastal marsh is found where streams meet the ocean in sheltered coves and small estuaries. Salt water from the ocean mixes with the fresh water from the streams to create flooded areas of brackish water, which provide a very productive habitat for wildlife. On Catalina, coastal marshes are called "salinas" and are quite different from mainland salt marshes in that they don't get inundated daily by tidal water. The best examples of salinas can be seen at Little Harbor, Catalina Harbor and Cherry Cove. The plants found in this habitat have a high tolerance to the harsh saline conditions and include coast weed (*Amblyopappus pusillus*), beach saltbush (*Atriplex leucophylla*), the introduced Australian saltbush (*Atriplex semibaccata*), Watson's saltbush (*Atriplex watsonii*), saltgrass (*Distichlis spicata*), alkali heath (*Frankenia grandifolia*), jaumea (*Jaumea carnosa*), salt cedar (*Monanthochloe littoralis*), the introduced sickle-grass (*Parapholis incurva*), pickleweed (*Salicornia subterminalis* and *S. virginica*), the impressive Pacific Coast bulrush (*Scirpus robustus*), coast sand spurrey (*Spergularia macrotheca*) and California sea blite (*Suaeda californica*). Salinas are also great places to look for wading birds.

Southern Beaches and Dunes

Beaches and sand dunes are very dynamic habitats. A beautiful sandy beach like the one at Little Harbor can be totally rebuilt overnight by a strong tide or a storm and then carved or shaped by waves and wind. But above the tideline, the dunes are a bit more stable, allowing colonization by herbaceous plants that can stand burial by the shifting sands. These plants tend to have long taproots and extensive root systems, which together give some permanence and stability to the dunes. On the mainland, dune habitats have almost disappeared due to coastal development, beach rebuilding, sand mining and especially heavy recreational use. On Catalina, these habitats are largely protected from undue disturbance. Great examples of this delicate habitat can be found at Little and Shark Harbors and at Ben Weston Beach. Characteristic species include the beautiful red sand verbena (*Abronia maritima*); silver beach bur (Ambrosia chamissonis); beach saltbush (*Atriplex leucophylla*); the introduced sea rocket (*Cakile maritima*), which is a species that

The red sand verbena grows well in loose sand and attracts insects to its purple/ red flowers. *Courtesy of Carlos de la Rosa.*

the conservancy controls with volunteer help; alkali weed (*Cressa truxillensis*); saltgrass (*Distichlis spicata*); and coast goldenbush (*Isocoma menziesii*).

Freshwater Habitats: Lakes, Ponds and Reservoirs

As dry as the island seems at times, there is fresh water to be found. However, most of the larger bodies of fresh water you may discover are man-made. In fact, there is only one natural lake on the island—Echo Lake, which dries up almost every year during the summer. All other ponds and lakes are actually

Cattails adorn the shore of Thompson Reservoir during sunset. *Courtesy of Carlos de la Rosa.*

man-made reservoirs built to support the now-defunct cattle industry. These are now very important to sustain the bison herd. The largest reservoir and one that seldom dries up is Thompson Reservoir in Middle Ranch. Other reservoirs include the Upper and Lower Buffalo Corrals Reservoirs, on the road to Two Harbors; Big Spring Reservoir; the small Buffalo Springs Reservoirs near the Airport in the Sky; Bulrush Reservoir; Cape Canyon Reservoir; and the photogenic and inviting Haypress Reservoir. Occasionally, one can find what are called "vernal pools," ephemeral accumulations of water that fill depressions in the landscape for a few weeks during the rainy season. Characteristic species of Catalina's pond and reservoir margins include redstem (*Ammannia robusta*), water starwort (*Callitriche marginata*), water pygmy weed (*Crassula aquatica*), California waterwort (*Elatine californica*), lowland cudweed (*Gnaphalium palustre*), meadow barley (*Hordeum brachyantherum californicum*), toad rush (*Juncus bufonius var. bufonius*), the introduced pondweeds (*Potamogeton crispus* and *P. pectinatus*), ditch grass (*Ruppia maritima*), vervain (*Verbena bracteata*) and cattails (*Typha spp.*). Pond edges are great places to see a number of species of dragonflies and damselflies, the males patrolling and defending territories, as well as a number of shorebirds. Bald eagles also like to perch and even nest near reservoirs, like the nest found at Thompson Reservoir.

Streams and Their Riparian Habitats

Streams on the island are unique and delicate habitats for wildlife. *Courtesy of Carlos de la Rosa.*

While most streams on Catalina are intermittent (meaning they only flow part of the year), some flow year-round, like Cottonwood Creek near Middle Ranch. The majority of streams flow only when there are rain events and are often called "arroyos." These riparian habitats are hugely important to most species on Catalina. Trees like black cottonwood (*Populus balsamifera var. trichocarpa*), the introduced California sycamore (*Platanus racemosa*) and willows (*Salix spp.*) are often accompanied by elderberry (*Sambucus mexicana*), Fremont cottonwood (*Populus fremontii*) and shrubs and vines such as mule fat (*Baccharis salicifolia*), California wild rose (*Rosa californica*), California blackberry (*Rubus ursinus*), snowberry (*Symphoricarpos mollis*), poison oak (*Toxicodendron diversilobum*), virgin's bower (*Clematis ligusticifolia*) and honeysuckle (*Lonicera spp.*). Herbaceous species typical of riparian communities include western ragweed (*Ambrosia psilostachya*), mugwort (*Artemisia douglasiana*), rye (*Elymus spp.*), yerba buena (*Satureja douglasii*), hoary nettle (*Urtica dioica holosericea*), vervain (*Verbena lasiostachys*) and cocklebur (*Xanthium spp.*). Along streams that dry up, one can find a herbaceous community composed mostly of cottonwoods (*Populus spp.*) and willows (*Salix spp.*). This habitat is dominated by such species as spiny rush (*Juncus acutus*) and cattails (*Typha spp.*) along with a variety of annual herbs and grasses. One unique and very special species of mammal found in these habitats is the endemic Catalina Island shrew (*Sorex ornatus willetti*), which is extremely rare and hard to find. It is actually one of the rarest mammals in North America!

Bugs, Bugs, Bugs Galore!

We didn't want to leave this section without mentioning the most diverse and species-rich group of organisms found on the island: the invertebrates. As is the case throughout most of the world, Catalina is home to an impressive number of species of insects and other invertebrates, many of them unique to the island (endemic). Every year, one or more new species are discovered on Catalina, some of them new to the island but many also new to science! The richness of habitats and plant species we described above form a great matrix for many invertebrates to exploit.

Most of the endemic species found on the island (more than sixty discovered so far) are invertebrates. There are at least seven species of land snails that

Endemic and waiting for a scientific name, the Catalina Jerusalem cricket awaits more scientific study. These crickets may be two species instead of just one! *Courtesy of Carlos de la Rosa.*

are unique to the island as well as fourteen species of beetles, five species of butterflies and moths, four species of crickets, one species of ant, one species of stick insect, one species of cicada, at least one species of fly, five species of bees and wasps, one species of spider, one species of centipede and one species of millipede. Compare that to five endemic species of mammals, three species of birds and eight species of plants and you'll realize how rich this group of animals is on the island. Invertebrates rule! Some groups, such as the aquatic insects, have not been studied on the island in any depth, so it is very possible that a number of new species could be discovered once researchers, with their nets and microscopes, take a closer look.

Among the most interesting species (for a bug-loving person, that is) are the beetles, of which new species to science have been discovered on Catalina as recently as 2010. Bees are also very important due to their roles as pollinators specializing on island plants. In total, there are at least 1,200 species of insects that have been collected and identified on Catalina, and there are many hundreds more to collect and add to the list. Catalina entomology is a great field of study and one that will continue to bring new species to science and add to the knowledge of the extraordinary ecology of the island.

We Are in a Hotspot

It's all well and good to say that Catalina is a unique and ecologically important place, but it never hurts to have one of the world's foremost authorities on such things make the case for you. Conservation International, a worldwide organization working on the conservation of the earth's biological resources, has defined what they consider to be the world's ecological hotspots—the richest and most threatened reservoirs of plant and animal life on earth. Their worldwide analysis lists twenty-five biodiversity hotspots around the world, including the California Floristic Province, which includes Catalina Island. These hotspots cover close to 12 percent of the planet's land surface but hold about 44 percent of the world's plants and 35 percent of all terrestrial vertebrates. Statistically, that means they are ecologically important at a level far disproportionate to their size. The other thing that makes them "hot" is that in most cases, these environments are under threat and shrinking in size. Therefore, if you want to save the largest portion of earth's remaining biodiversity, focusing on the hotspots, where unique things exist and are under threat, makes a whole lot of sense. It's a bigger bang for your buck, so to speak.

Catalina Island, as part of the California Floristic Province, holds many unique species. Threats to the floristic province include development, invasive species, deforestation and conversion from wild to urban or agricultural uses. While it's somewhat customary for ecologists to dwell on doom-and-gloom scenarios, we're quite pleased to be able to take this conversation in an entirely different direction.

Unlike most of the world's hotspots, Catalina may not only be slowing but reversing the trend toward ecological decay. The ecology of Catalina is actually in far better shape today than it was one hundred years ago or even a decade ago. The odds are high that it will be in better shape yet ten years from now!

Why is it that Catalina is faring so well when so many others are not? With 88 percent of Catalina Island owned and protected by the Catalina Island Conservancy, loss of natural land and habitat is no longer a major issue. And the conservancy doesn't just own the land, they manage it by removing invasive species, protecting sensitive plants and wildlife and managing threats to the ecosystem as they arise. As a result, Catalina's habitats are coming back, and that represents hope for hotspots everywhere. Even the worst ecological issues can be solved. As we like to say, all it takes is money, a plan and a whole lot of work.

Where There Is No Carpenter, the Plumber Builds the Furniture: Niches and Unique Ecological Roles

In addition to the isolation and evolutionary issues we've covered, one of the more interesting aspects of island ecology is that some species that would normally play certain ecological roles in a landscape simply never arrive to do the job. This leaves vacant niches. Essentially, a niche is how an organism goes about making a living within its ecosystem. If a niche is "empty" or available, it presents an opportunity for a new species to move into that role. Empty niches rarely stay empty for long.

Take, for example, dung beetles. Dung beetles play a huge role in breaking down and burying the large amounts of fecal matter produced by large herbivores in mainland ecosystems. In some cases, these specialized beetles can find and begin breaking down big piles of dung just minutes after they hit the ground. This kind of nutrient cycling is really important because it ensures that valuable natural energy makes its way back into a useable form as fast as possible. But large dung beetles never settled on Catalina. This isn't shocking when you consider that Catalina has no large native herbivores. Our Catalina California ground squirrels are the largest, and they have a head the size of a walnut and produce relatively small droppings.

But in the 1920s, bison were introduced to Catalina. They're not from here, and they'd never be able to swim the channel or float over on a mat of vegetation. But suddenly, thanks to the wonders of modern transportation, they drop in unannounced and, from the ecology's standpoint, uninvited. As we're starting to see, species don't exist in a vacuum. The interaction of species connects all things together so that the ecosystem can function. On the mainland, all of those pieces are in place and the ecology is complete. On the Great Plains of North America, where there have always been big piles of dung, you can be sure that something evolved to take advantage of the free but rather disgusting lunch. The Great Plains are home to a variety of dung beetles perfectly equipped to break down every pile. Not so on Catalina. And one thing about bison is that they're really, really good at producing dung. That leads to the question: with no big dung beetles on Catalina, how does the stuff get broken down and recycled?

It goes something like this. Suddenly, there's a new open niche, a veritable poop-a-palooza, and there are lots of nutrients that nobody else is taking advantage of. In the absence of specialists, new (and less qualified) species wade in to take advantage of the situation. But most beetles with even a passing interest in poop on Catalina are rather small in size. That makes sense since they'd have evolved to make a living off of droppings they'd come in contact with. In this case, that would mean relatively small fox, squirrel or mouse droppings. While the little dung-loving creatures are able to take advantage of this new resource, they're not specialists, and as a result they do a less-than-perfect job of things. The end product of all this, if you will, is that bison droppings on Catalina tend to persist.

Is it possible that, over time, a dung beetle will arrive on a mat of floating vegetation and get to work—or that one of our existing beetles may create a better way to take advantage of the patties? Given enough time, it seems likely, but for now, things on the ground level are out of balance. Nutrients dropped by foxes or squirrels can be rapidly cycled back into the system. Nutrients dropped by bison are stalled for a time due to the lack of specialists around to do the job properly. But at least the process is getting done, albeit inefficiently. Sun, wind, rain and yes, little dung beetles, eventually work on the big dung piles and break them down, but it takes a lot longer than normal. In situations like this, the jobs of specialists are performed by generalists. Over time, the generalists may evolve to become specialists and in the process become a new species or subspecies. That actually happens rather frequently. It's just one more set of circumstances that makes Catalina unique.

Chapter 5

HUMANS

Up to this point, humans have been noticeably absent from the scene. Catalina formed, rose from the sea, filled with life and evolved into a fully functional and amazing ecosystem—all without the presence of human beings. You might anticipate this being the part of the book in which we switch from visions of an island "ecotopia" and rain down pestilence and devastation at the hand of man, but you'd be mistaken. There's a tendency to think of humans as different or separate from nature, but this isn't actually the case. Modern life has certainly given us the ability to pretend that we're somehow separate from our ecologies, but we're not, and we never will be. We're as reliant on Mother Nature as we've ever been. It's just that from inside our heated buildings and fast cars, it's sometimes easy to forget—until the cost of gas or heating oil goes up. But back in what we call "pristine times," humans were directly and collectively connected to the land in a way that was in harmony with natural systems. We lived within the confines of what nature provided. We ate only what we could kill or collect, and we could catch and collect only what we could personally put our hands on or bring down with an arrow or spear. We were natural. Catalina's first human inhabitants, the Tongva, were those kind of people.

When Humans Were One with the Land

Imagine Catalina, fully formed, ecology in place, with a wild coastline and thriving marine environment. It was during this time, some nine to twelve thousand years ago, that a group of humans arrived by boat and climbed ashore to find a place of remarkable potential. These people were the Tongva. They named their island Pimu and are sometimes referred to as Pimugnans. The Tongva are also often referred to as Gabrielinos, and though many names can be found in the literature, we'll stick with Tongva. Our Tongva friends tell us that they prefer it, as Pumugnan and Gabrielino were names assigned to them by Europeans. Gabrielino, incidentally, arose from the time the Tongva spent at the San Gabriel Mission well after Europeans arrived on Catalina. As you'll see, the San Gabriel years were not the best of times for the Tongva.

By all accounts, it appears that the Tongva came to North America from the ocean and worked their way from island to island toward the mainland. There's even evidence that North America's First People may have come by sea, following the bounty supplied by kelp beds along the coast often referred to as the "Kelp Highway." Though we're focusing on the Southern Channel Islands, it's worth mentioning that another group, the Chumash, was inhabiting the Northern Channel Islands at this time. The two groups were socially, culturally and geographically distinct. A bit of creative web surfing will lead you to some good information on the Chumash, who are an amazing people and worthy of a closer look. We also recommend checking out the Northern Channel Island National Park, the Santa Barbara Museum of Natural History and the Fowler Museum at UCLA as good, reliable sources.

For the Tongva, each of the Southern Channel Islands they encountered would have been very different and would have offered up different opportunities. Life on San Nicolas would have been different than life on Catalina, and life on Santa Barbara Island would have been very different than life on San Clemente. The ecology of each of the Channel Islands would have dramatically influenced the lifestyles, cultures and population densities of their inhabitants. Even then people were defined by their locales. The Tongva would have had friends and relatives on other islands as well as the mainland, and we know that they were outstanding boaters who moved around with relative ease. But if you lived on Pimu, the odds are that you spent most of your time there—you were Pimugnan.

As humans do, the Tongva began to explore after arriving on Pimu. They discovered plentiful springs and clean water, an amazing marine environment filled with good food, a people-friendly climate and relative safety, along with plenty of protected coves. In short, they found a place they would be happy to call home. As humans also do, the Tongva brought things with them when they arrived. They brought technologies such as boats, the ability to craft fishing hooks from shells, nets and more, and they found ways to use Catalina stone, minerals and driftwood to make those technologies work on their new island home.

It also looks like they brought something else to the island that is still here today: the Catalina Island fox. It's technically possible that the foxes could have made their way here on floating mats of vegetation, although it seems unlikely. For one thing, they would have been too large to have remained buoyed, fed and watered for the trip. For another, there's the not-so-coincidental coincidence that the arrival of foxes to each of the Channel Islands corresponds with arrival of the Tongva. On Catalina, it appears that foxes arrived somewhere around nine to twelve thousand years ago—same as the Tongva. Why would the Tongva be carting foxes around from island to island? Fur? Food? Companionship? We like the fur and companionship theories. Fur would have been a very useful thing to have, and as far as companionship, island foxes would have been pretty adorable. We're told that fox meat would not be very palatable. We may never know for sure, but whatever the reasons, it's clear that the Tongva liked having foxes around.

Of the eight California Channel Islands, six of them are large enough to sustain island fox populations. Each of these six islands—Catalina, San Nicolas, San Clemente, San Miguel, Santa Rosa and Santa Cruz—has foxes, but here's the interesting thing: each island's fox species has evolved to become a distinct subspecies, separate from the others. This is evolution by isolation in action. Since the foxes don't exchange genes from island to island, each population would have rapidly diverged, driven by their specific genetic potential and the ecological character of their island. The evolution of six subspecies in fewer than twelve thousand years would be almost unheard of for a mainland species. As we hope we've made abundantly clear, things operate differently on islands.

We often get the question: "If foxes were introduced by the Tongva, why do we consider them a native species? I mean, they were introduced, right?" The answer is a definitive: "Well, kind of only sort of." Remember at the beginning of the chapter when we talked about humans living in harmony with their environment? If you're a native behaving within the laws of the natural system around you, your capacity to create an offense to the environment is lower. It's not zero, but it's limited. Since this particular introduction occurred prior to the arrival of the Europeans, we generally consider it as normal. You can find arguments on both sides of this issue, but unless you consider human beings as a species that was never in harmony with the natural world, this argument has merit. The Tongva also brought dogs to Catalina and almost certainly quail and the valley oak. Introductions like this make for interesting conversations about what's really native to Catalina, but in modern times, we don't struggle as much with the distinction of when an "introduced" species is unnatural. There are so many non-native and invasive species arriving on islands that our biggest issue is dealing with the potential for them to decimate the natural systems we're trying to protect. For example, raccoons stowing away on yachts and jumping off when they reach the island are a serious problem in Catalina. They are not and will never be native to Catalina. Ditto for deer, fennel, Canary Island or flax-leaved broom and more than two hundred species of plants and animals that are considered non-native on Catalina.

After a time, the Tongva also began to move a few things off of Catalina. Their primary and perhaps most important discovery and export was soapstone, or steatite. It's the one true Tongva economic export, and pieces made in Catalina have been found as far east as Colorado. What's so special about soapstone? You can carve a bowl from it, fill it full of food and water, set it right into the fire and take it out when the food's done. If you've ever spent much time around a campfire, you know that virtually all other rocks break when you remove them from the fire and let them cool quickly. Not so with soapstone. It's got a high talc content, which allows it to expand and contract without breaking up. Soapstone is also very easy to carve into almost anything you want, so most any size or shape of bowl could be fashioned to suit most any need. It was also great for carving figurines into all shapes and sizes. Archaeologists have found soapstone carved into net weights, hooks, pendants, totems bowls and all kinds of jewelry. There's a terrific soapstone quarry near Catalina's Airport in the Sky that shows evidence of their mining technique on a rock face. Here you can see half-excavated soapstone bowls sitting just as the Tongva left them when they began moving off the island.

But in terms of cooking, soapstone was to other rocks what the microwave oven is to the conventional oven. It must have been one of those discoveries that, once you found it, you wondered how you ever got along without it. More than just a new type of cookware, soapstone represented a major social advancement. The Tongva could now make stews and soups and other highly nutritious dishes that were really hard to pull off prior to soapstone, and that

This soapstone quarry near Catalina's Airport in the Sky shows bowls in mid-production, exactly as the Tongva left them. *Courtesy of Frank J. Hein.*

meant they could get every available nutrient out of every bit of fish, acorn, bulb or fruit. More nutrition meant greater health, and greater health meant better chances of survival. The Tongva also used woven baskets filled with hot rocks to heat water, and so soapstone wasn't all they had. But it's not an overstatement to say that the development of soapstone bowls and utensils was a life-altering advancement for the Tongva—so much so that the word got out. Soapstone bowls from Catalina have been found as far away as Colorado and show up routinely along Native American trade routes in the West. It was as big a deal economically as it was socially.

Chapter 6
YOU'RE NOT FROM AROUND HERE, ARE YOU?

In North American history, we generally make the distinction of "pre-European" and "post-European," and this is for a good reason. Before Europeans found North America, civilizations here were living close to the land—though it should be noted that they did manipulate the land to increase their quality of life. Most of the plants and animals on Catalina were native. How could they be otherwise? While there's plenty of evidence to show that humans were impacting their environment even back in pre-European times, those impacts usually allowed for systems to recover, thrive and achieve sustainability.

Archeological evidence from middens (places where the Tongva discarded their refuse) shows that abalone shells in the later days of the Tongva were smaller on average than shells from thousands of years prior. Harvesting was clearly impacting abalone populations but not decimating them. The Tongva's impact pales in comparison to our current capacity to dive deep with scuba gear or trawl the oceans with massive nets. We can now harvest species at rates and locations the Tongva could never have imagined, and our current capacity to alter the environment is quite capable of destroying entire ecologies.

While the Tongva lived on Catalina for thousands of years before Europeans came onto the scene, one can still find references to the Spanish "discovering" the island. It's as hilarious as it is tragic, but it does reveal the mindset of Europeans at the time, one that is still referred to in history books. These lands, along with their potential riches, were there

Items found in middens are a gold mine for archaeologists seeking to understand the lives and habits of Catalina's first people. *Courtesy of Carlos de la Rosa.*

just waiting to be taken—no matter that they were already occupied by Native Peoples.

Be that as it may, the Spanish did manage to find Pimu—Tongva and all—back in the 1500s. They immediately claimed it for Spain, as was the custom of the time. On October 1542, Juan Rodriguez Cabrillo found Catalina while exploring the California coast and named it San Salvador, after his ship. On that same trip, he also named and claimed San Diego and Santa Barbara Island, as well as a few other choice properties. Shortly thereafter in 1543, Cabrillo died of complications from a broken leg, and rumor has it that he's buried on either Catalina or San Miguel Island. His actual burial site has never been conclusively identified, but nonetheless there is a monument dedicated to him on San Miguel Island amidst a beautiful forest of giant coreopsis (yes, another giant). Whether he's buried there or not, it's a beautiful place and well worth a visit if you're lucky enough to make the trip.

On November 24, 1602, Sebastian Vizcaino "rediscovered" the island while exploring and mapping the California coastline. Since

This image, taken on the island of San Miguel, shows a marker commemorating Juan Rodriquez Cabrillo. It is believed that he was buried on either San Miguel or Santa Catalina, but we may never know for sure. *Courtesy of Frank J. Hein.*

November 24 was the eve of Saint Catherine's Day, he named the island Isla Santa Catalina. The name stuck.

WHAT THE SPANISH ENCOUNTERED

Upon landing on Catalina, both Vizcaino and Cabrillo found the Tongva living what was by all measures a pretty comfortable and civilized existence. There were settlements in what's now Avalon, Two Harbors, Little Harbor and many, many points in between. Just about every cove had a settlement or village, and there were also many villages and inhabited places in the interior of the island, including "industrial" sites close to outcrops of soapstone and near springs. Conservative estimates suggest that well over two thousand Tongva were living on Catalina at any given time. The sea provided a plentiful bounty, and the land provided bulbs and other nutritious plants as well as fresh water and building materials. The Tongva had the technology to dry and store food for lean times and were even cooking up some serious meals with their state-of-the-art soapstone cookery. They also carried vast amounts of whole abalone deep into the interior of the island, as evidenced by the piles of shells found in middens far from the shore. These abalone could have easily provided fresh food to workers and interior villagers for a few days.

All of this must have surprised the Spanish, who would have no doubt been expecting an encounter with a primitive culture. Instead they discovered that the Tongva were socially advanced and friendly, living the kind of modern existence that would have seemed familiar, right down to the character of the Tongva villages. Their houses, which they called "Ki" or "Ki-ish," were often lined up much like homes on a modern street. The Tongva had a formal government structure, currency, art, industry and more. If they were "primitive" people, it would have been news to the Tongva.

The Tongva were also accomplished ocean travelers. They built large canoes called Ti'ats using wooden planks and caulked the gaps with asphaltum, a tar that washed ashore from underwater seeps. That's right— the Tongva were taking advantage of petroleum products thousands of years before we figured it out. Holding up to twelve people, the Ti'at was a marvelous vessel that allowed the Tongva to travel to and from other Channel Islands and the mainland, visiting friends and family and trading

Avalon from the air. It's a beautiful island and a lovely town, and nature is never more than a short stroll away. *Courtesy of Carlos de la Rosa.*

The Bell Chimes Tower, just a short stroll from downtown Avalon, still rings on the hour just as it's done since 1925, when it was presented as a gift from Mrs. Ada Wrigley to the Town of Avalon. *Courtesy of Terri Bassett.*

Kayak trips like this one, launched from Descanso Beach, can get you close to nature even when your time on the island is short. *Courtesy of Carlos de la Rosa.*

Not your average squirrel. Catalina is home to just one species of squirrel, the Catalina California ground squirrel, and this one's special—it's evolved to become an island giant. *Courtesy of Carlos de la Rosa.*

A stop at the Avalon Canyon Nature Center is a must if you're looking to learn about wild Catalina. You'll find it on your way to the Wrigley Memorial and Botanical Gardens. *Courtesy of Kelly Callaghan.*

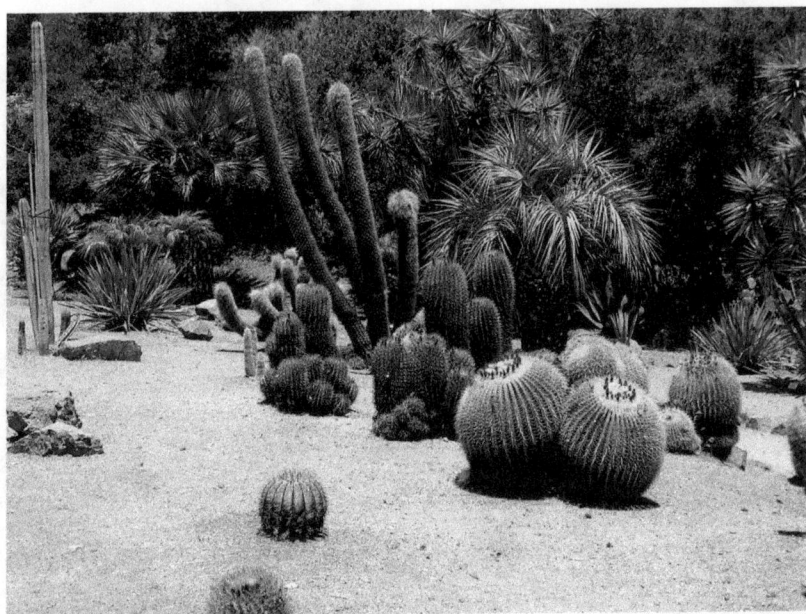

What began as a personal collection of the Wrigley family grew to become a full-scale botanic garden. Exotic cacti from around the world, as well as Catalina's rarest and most exotic plants, can be found here. *Courtesy of Frank Hein.*

The Wrigley Memorial, on the grounds of the botanic gardens, was once the resting place of William Wrigley Jr. The view from the top of the memorial is spectacular. For even better views, take the "Garden to Sky Hike," which begins from here. *Courtesy of Terri Bassett.*

Sure, it looks like any other quail, but like so many things on Catalina, this one's special. Another island giant, quail on Catalina are not hunted, and large coveys can be found roaming from Avalon to Two Harbors and beyond. *Courtesy of Tyler Dvorak.*

Above: The Hogsback Gate is as far as you can go by golf cart, but there are a variety of ecotours tours available year-round, and with a permit, you can hike and bike at your leisure. *Courtesy of Frank Hein.*

Left: The road beyond Hogsback Gate can be steep, winding and, as seen here, foggy. Locals say that no two trips to the summit or the wildlands are ever the same. *Courtesy of Frank Hein.*

Above: Bison calves are adorable and, on Catalina, less common now that the herd is managed using an innovative birth control technique. This approach allows the Catalina Island Conservancy to keep this non-native species at numbers low enough to protect the environment but high enough that visitors can experience them in the wild. *Courtesy of Julie King.*

Left: Charismatic bison roam Catalina's wildlands, making do with the grasses the island has to offer. The landmass in the background is the Palos Verdes Peninsula. *Courtesy of Frank Hein.*

This verdant landscape between the summit and the Airport in the Sky shows how slight differences in the slope of the land can make the difference between green and lush or brown and dry. *Courtesy of Terri Bassett.*

Voted one of the "World's Most Thrilling Airports," Catalina's Airport in the Sky is a great destination even if you're not flying in. Whether you're up for hiking, biking or a relaxing lunch while you take in the view, the airport's a good bet. Transportation options abound. *Courtesy of Carlos de la Rosa.*

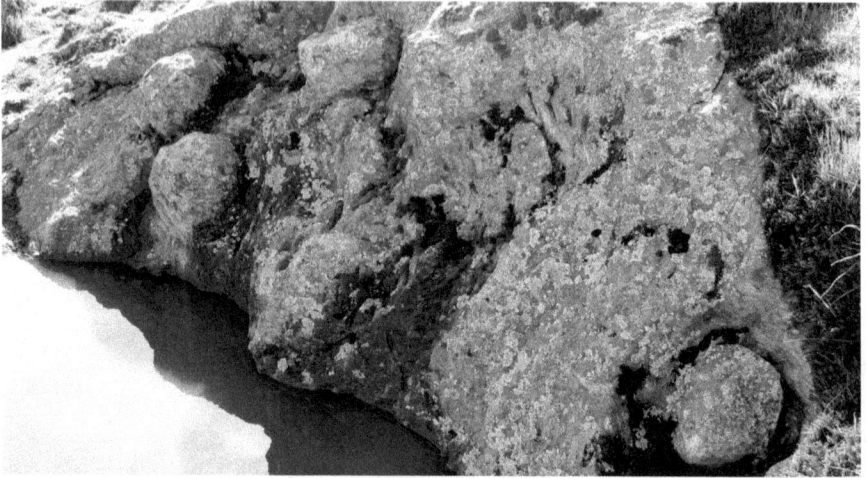

If you find yourself at the airport, be sure to take the very short hike to the soapstone quarry, where you can see soapstone bowls in the process of being quarried, just as the Tongva left them. The outsides of the bowls were formed in place before being "struck" off the wall so that the insides could be hollowed out by hand. *Courtesy of Frank Hein.*

This wild Catalina Island fox, shown here with a newly attached radio collar, is part of a recovery effort that's working. As a result of an outbreak of canine distemper in 1999, there were fewer than 100 foxes on Catalina. As of 2013, the population had rebounded to more than 1,500. Not out of the woods yet, the Catalina Island fox remains a federally listed endangered species. *Courtesy of Julie King.*

Tachi on the prowl. Until her passing in December 2012, Tachi served as an ambassador for her species. In her time on Catalina, she helped raise funding and awareness for the Catalina Island Fox Recovery Program. With the fox population now in excess of pre-crash numbers, her work is done. *Courtesy of Carlos de la Rosa.*

The Santa Catalina Island Vineyard at El Rancho Escondido. Little Harbor is visible at the bottom of the ridge. *Courtesy of Carlos de la Rosa.*

Little Harbor, with its calm waters, and Shark Harbor, with its pounding surf, offer a classic Catalina shoreline experience. The entrance to Two Harbors via Cat Harbor is visible at the top left of the image. *Courtesy of Carlos de la Rosa.*

The sleepy town of Two Harbors is the island's "other" population center. With its laid-back attitude, fewer than three hundred year-round residents and an active boating community, it's a great place to unwind. *Courtesy of Terri Bassett.*

Catalina's "Wild West End" from the air. With its rugged landscape and coastline, the west end is home to the island's most remote and challenging nature experiences. *Courtesy of Carlos de la Rosa.*

The west end can also be accessed via numerous boat-in campsites. The leeward shores are also home to a variety of camps where literally millions of youth have come for life-changing experiences. The camps are a critical component of Catalina's cultural fabric. *Courtesy of Carlos de la Rosa.*

Top: The Avalon hairstreak (*Strymon avalona*) is a Catalina Island endemic, meaning that it's found here and nowhere else. At current count, there are over sixty-four endemic species and subspecies on Catalina, with more being discovered every year. *Courtesy of Carlos de la Rosa.*

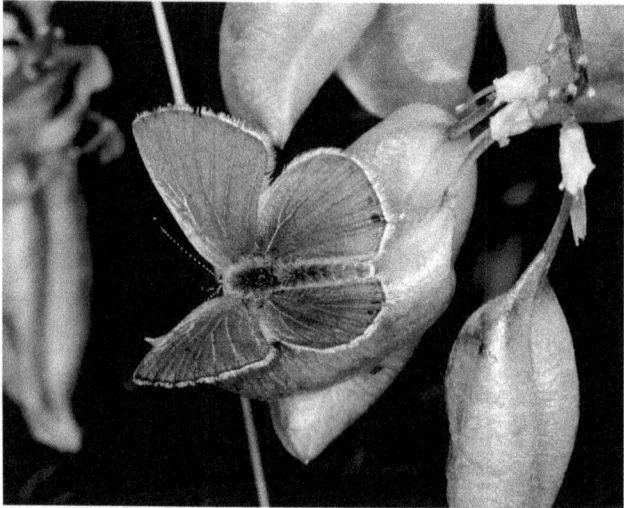

Middle: This western-tailed blue butterfly (*Everes amyntula*) shimmers against a background of green. *Courtesy of Carlos de la Rosa.*

Bottom: Looking like an alien from another planet, this Jerusalem cricket is endemic to Catalina. Still waiting to receive a scientific name, it's another example of the strange and wonderful diversity that islands can foster. *Courtesy of Carlos de la Rosa.*

Got pollen? You can see how effective insects can be at moving pollen around the island, and it's a good thing. Without the arrival of pollinators, life on Catalina would not be the same. *Courtesy of Carlos de la Rosa.*

This hillside comes alive with a splash of yellow each spring as bush sunflowers burst out in bloom. *Courtesy of Frank Hein.*

This field of island poppies, bluedicks and bright green grasses offers up a rainbow palette. Wildflower season varies from year to year, but if you time it right, a springtime hike can be a very colorful experience. *Courtesy of Carlos de la Rosa.*

This female American kestrel frequents Catalina's open country. Although it's North America's smallest falcon, it's a voracious eater. Watch for them perched on wires or hovering over grasslands. Odds are good that you'll see one pounce on an unsuspecting bug or mouse. Don't forget to pack your binoculars! *Courtesy of Tyler Dvorak.*

Named after the Wrigley family, the USC Wrigley Institute for Environmental Studies directly and through its partners offers a wide variety of world-class ocean and environmental programs. *Courtesy of Carlos de la Rosa.*

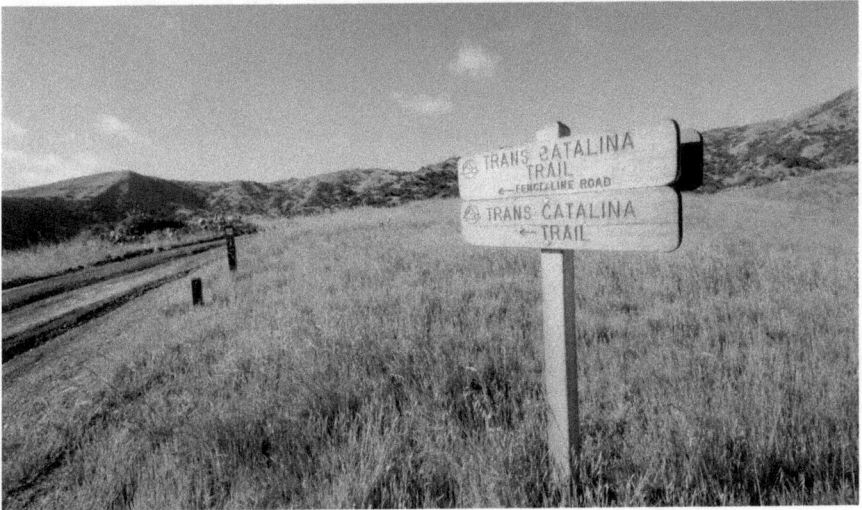

Opened in 2009, the Trans-Catalina Trail provides visitors with an incredible opportunity to hike and camp across the length of Catalina Island. At just over thirty-seven miles long, it's a serious challenge. But take heart—you can hike as much or as little as you like. *Courtesy of Carlos de la Rosa.*

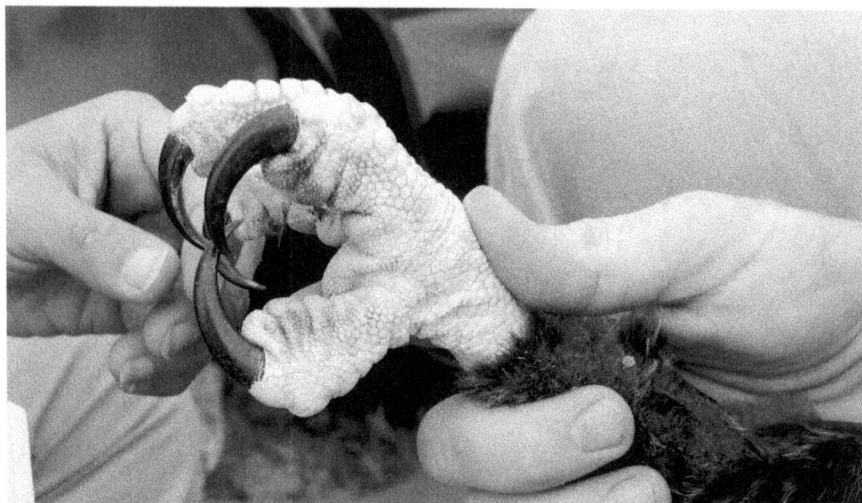

My, what big talons you have! Working with bald eagles has its risks, but through the work of the Institute for Wildlife Studies (the hand on the left) and the Catalina Island Conservancy (the hand on the right), bald eagles are once again flourishing on Catalina! *Courtesy of Frank Hein.*

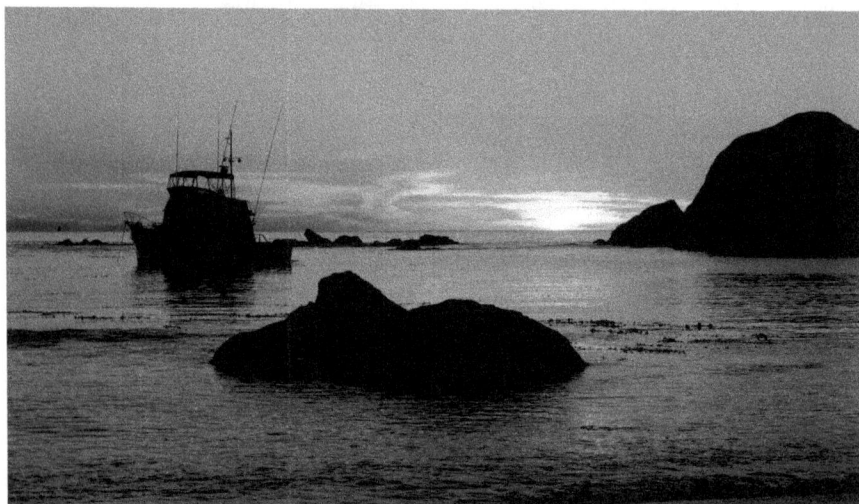

The sun never sets in Avalon. It's one of the very few places in North America where you can stand on the shore, face the ocean and watch the sun rise! This sunset was taken miles away from Little Harbor, looking west. *Courtesy of Terri Bassett.*

soapstone tools and bowls and other goods. Currently, the Ti'at Society keeps alive the Tongva's maritime traditions through exhibits and an annual event in which today's tribe members make crossings from the mainland to the Channel Islands exactly as their ancestors did. This is probably a good time to mention that the Tongva are still around, and we have the privilege of meeting and working with them from time to time. As they like to say, "We're still here." It's a good thing to remember.

Change Accelerates

Now even if the Spanish weren't interested in conquering the Tongva, the fate of the tribe was pretty well sealed as soon as the two cultures met. Historically, when Europeans crossed paths with aboriginal peoples, things ended badly for the home team. While the nature of conflict between Europeans and North American native cultures is complicated enough to fill a book (such as Jared Diamond's brilliant treatise on the subject, *Guns, Germs and Steel*), we're going to simplify things a bit—okay, a lot. When cultures clash, the ones that have the guns fare better. However, there's a more formidable weapon that comes along for the ride: disease. When you live in relative isolation as the Tongva did, you're susceptible to germs, viruses and diseases that are new to you. Europeans had been living and raising animals in close proximity to each other and traveling the world for years, and in the process they encountered and built up immunity to a dizzying array of germs, viruses and parasites, all new to the isolated Tongva.

When the Europeans arrived from far-flung places and set foot on the shores of relatively isolated places, where immunity to these diseases simply didn't exist, things weren't going to go well. We know that new strains of bad things entered the lives of the Tongva shortly after European arrival. Not only did the European sailors carry with them a number of diseases and parasites (which found a fresh host in the Tongva) such as smallpox, typhus, cholera and measles, but they also carried loads of rats and mice in their ships, which themselves were carriers of diseases and germs. The arrival of rats and mice to islands makes for a complex story, affecting not only humans that would come into contact with them but also wreaking havoc on colonies of seabirds and competing with the few native species of rodents. Rat- and mice-borne diseases such as hantavirus, tularemia, leptospirosis, plague and others would have caused rapid changes in the island's ecology. All of this was bad news for the Tongva.

By and large, the Spanish explored the island; made some notes about what they found; took some time to repair their boats, pick up supplies and pass along a few viruses, germs, rats and mice; and moved on in search of greater riches and other places to conquer. As first contacts go, it was a relatively tame encounter.

It was in the late 1700s and early 1800s that the Tongva's luck really began to run out. Out there, somewhere over the horizon, the Russians were coming, accompanied by Aleut fur hunters. Word had gotten out that the Channel Islands were home to large populations of sea otters just waiting to be harvested and taken to market. The road to riches for the Russians and Aleuts consisted of a brutally simple plan: kill as many fur-bearers as you could as fast as you could and when you've taken what there is to take, get back to port and cash out. They were chillingly effective. In just a few short years, they'd decimated the sea otter populations in Southern California to the point that they've still not recovered. The impact on the Tongva, who would have relied on meat and fur from this species, was immediate and long lasting, and they didn't much care for what was going on.

Where initial contact between the Tongva and newly arriving Europeans had to this point been more or less cordial, interactions between the fur traders and the Tongva were getting downright ugly. At the time the fur traders arrived on San Nicolas, the Tongva's there (sometimes called Nicoleños) numbered around three hundred. The Nicoleños opposed the hunts, as they understood that their livelihood was being threatened. Opposition turned to anger, anger to skirmishes and ultimately to at least one very bloody fight that left nearly all of the Nicoleño men dead. By the time the fur traders had moved on, there were fewer than twenty Nicoleños left on the island, and the Tongva era on San Nicolas gradually drew to an end. The remaining Nicoleños appear to have been relocated to mainland missions in the 1820s, and their culture never recovered. The Tongva on Pimu experienced a related but less well-documented fate.

Imagine you're a Tongva living on Pimu (Catalina) or any of the other Channel Islands and you hear of these events unfolding. What would you do? The Tongva could have read the writing on the wall and they would have reacted. Almost certainly, some families began to move themselves out of harm's way, with the intent, no doubt, of returning when things got back to normal. Precise details of the decline of Channel Island tribes aren't universally agreed upon, but we do know this much is true: as European

Islanders assist archaeologists from the Pimu Catalina Island Archaeology Project as they explore one of the many sites on Catalina. *Courtesy Frank J. Hein.*

contact increased, native tribes decreased in size and cultural stability until a point where the last of the Tongva and Chumash were ferried off of their island homes to mainland missions or left of their own accord. By the mid- to late 1820s, Channel Island native cultures were either decimated or marginalized, and the fate of the islands fell to European influence. By the 1900s, the Tongva's original language was all but lost, as were many of their traditional beliefs and mythology, which fell to the relentless Christianization implemented by the Spanish. However, remnants of their language can still be found today. Names such as Pimu, Pacoima, Tujunga, Topanga, Rancho Cucamonga, Azusa and Cahuenga Pass are indelibly stamped on the land and remind us of the Tongva heritage. The life the Tongva had known and treasured slipped away in much the same way it was slipping away for Native Americans across the continent.

Before we leave the Tongva, let's take one last look at how remarkable they were. The modern-day population of Catalina is somewhere around

3,800 residents. Current estimates of Catalina in the Tongva era range from 2,000 to 3,000. Imagine that the barges that now bring food, drink, supplies and fuel to the island on a daily basis suddenly stop running and the people are left to fend for themselves. Now come back in a couple years and take a guess at how many island residents would still be here. But the Tongva nearly matched our numbers and kept their people fed, sheltered and thriving using just the resources that the island and ocean provided. To accomplish this, they would have had to be masters of their ecology, knowing where every edible plant lived, when it was ready to harvest and how to harvest them sustainably. They would have known where every spring was located, where mineral deposits could be found, where the best abalone beds were found, how and when to catch fish and so much more. It would be nice to know now what they knew then, but aside from some really outstanding archeological and anthropological research being done, that opportunity has been lost. It is a shame on too many levels to count.

Today's archaeological work on Catalina Island is slow and cautious, following closely the parameters set by agreements with modern Tongva, whose traditions and beliefs are respected and honored. For example, burial sites are considered sacred places of rest for their ancestors, and these shall remain undisturbed and protected. The methods of early archaeologists to dig up burial grounds in search of "treasure" and artifacts, often desecrating the human remains they found, are things of a painful past. Working closely with Tongva archaeologists, modern researchers and their students focus on surface discoveries; mapping the remaining artifacts, villages and burial sites; and studying existing artifacts preserved in official museums and collections. We learn from our past mistakes, and this new generation of archaeologists and scholars is adding pieces to the stories with respect and sensitivity to the cultures that so greatly influenced the story of Catalina Island.

Chapter 7
IT'S A LIVING

Mining, Ranching, Ownership and the Advent of Tourism

For dozens of reasons, humans have always found Catalina a compelling place to live. That was as true for the Tongva as it was for all humans who followed. For most of its human history, Catalina was relatively stable, with new visitors being infrequent. However, that relative stability pretty much went off the rails in the late 1800s, when new waves of visitors began to arrive on its shores. And with these visitors came a series of changes that would gradually lead us to the Catalina we know today. From a historical perspective, Catalina was becoming a happening place, which was arguably better for the newcomers than it was for the original inhabitants.

As we look at the ways in which new arrivals transformed Catalina, it's both necessary and interesting to take a look at the economics of Catalina over the course of history. This is an exploration of the lengths that settlers would go to in order to make a life for themselves on an island that had all the makings of a paradise.

Around the mid-1800s, the fur traders, having taken all that they could take, moved on, leaving the social and cultural fabric of the Channel Islands in disarray. At this time, the rest of western North America was also being "discovered," and a steady flow of people were fanning across the Great Plains. Wave upon wave of settlers spilled out across the west into the "land

7,000-14,000 years ago	Tongva people settle the island. They lived within the carrying capacity of the island, though they did alter the landscape/ecologies.
1562 and 1602-	The Spanish arrive introducing pathogens but water scarcity makes the Island of little interest.
1800-	Otter hunters show up wipe out marine mammal populations
1840's-	Goats and sheep introduced for Farming. Ranching.
1860's-	Mining attempts begin
1880's-	Catalina is developed for tourism
1919	The Wrigleys Purchase Catalina Island
1930's-	Catalina tourism focuses on recreation, Hunting; enter pigs and deer
1970's-	Conservancy takes control of 88% of the land to protect island ecosystems
1990's-	Feral Herbivore removal programs begin, endangered species work continues, conservation work accelerates
2000's-	Ecotourism begins to grow. Invasive plant management begins.

A table of major milestones in Catalina's human history. Note how rapidly change accelerates upon the arrival of Europeans. *Courtesy Frank J. Hein.*

of opportunity," and rapid change became the new norm. Standing on the western coastline gazing out at the sea from a turbulent little border town named Los Angeles, Catalina Island would have been clearly visible to any and all. And for those with a restless spirit and a taste for exploration, Catalina's draw would have been irresistible. It was just a matter of time before the curious and adventurous began sailing for Catalina with business in their minds.

And sail they did. Ships began to moor in Catalina's harbors on a regular basis. Most were just curious visitors who came and left, but there were those immediately seized with the desire to stay and make Catalina their home. The reason for this is pretty simple: Catalina was and still is a nice place to live. It's remote, but not so remote that you can't get here and back with a decent boat. With apologies to Los Angelinos, even in the 1840s Catalina was seen as a paradise compared to Los Angeles and the other rowdy frontier towns of the mainland. The idea of escaping to Catalina had a certain romantic appeal.

Much like today, the island's unspoiled coastline, thriving marine environment, wild backcountry and strangely wonderful isolation made it the kind of place that begged you to stay awhile. The trick was in finding a way to make a living here. The economics of making a living on the island were complex and challenging. It cost a lot to ship everything you needed over from the mainland. Reliable and plentiful fresh water was tough to come by, and the land was steep and rugged. There were no roads either, which made getting around a challenge to say the least. Now if we'd really paid attention to how the Tongva had pulled things off for all those years, we could have learned from them and saved ourselves a whole lot of grief. But as we know from the history books, out here in the Wild West, we Americans kind of like to do things our own way.

In any event, the next one hundred years or so were driven by the innate human desire to make Catalina work, and the task was set upon with classic American determination. We'll detail several major economic models that were attempted, starting in the 1800s and leading to the present day. As we explore these models, we'll also describe the impacts these activities have had on the vulnerable and irreplaceable ecosystems of Catalina.

After the fur-trading episode, a series of new economic models began to bloom on Catalina. Around 1849, the word got out that Catalina might be gold country, and squatters from all over made the journey to Catalina to stake their claims and try their luck. While this was the main attraction for a new wave of adventurers to Catalina, the gold rush also brought with it a number of entrepreneurs with other ideas for the island.

The gold era on Catalina was a disappointment and fizzled a few short years after it began. Gold was found but in rather insignificant amounts, and it wasn't worth the trouble of getting to it and extracting it. However, other minerals like silver, lead and zinc were also found, and these discoveries eventually led to the development of a mining period on the island that spanned from 1863 until 1927. We can still see the remnants of the mine shafts, mounds of mine tailings on the way to Blackjack and some of the artifacts left behind from this effort both at Blackjack and Eagle's Nest Lodge near Middle Ranch.

Around this same time, ranchers were also trying their hand on Catalina. It's easy to understand why Catalina seemed like an ideal place to raise sheep, cattle and horses. For would-be ranchers, Catalina was blessed with a lack of large predators. There were no coyotes, wolves, bears or mountain lions to make a meal out of your defenseless livestock—all you had to do was let your animals roam and eat to their heart's content and take care of some veterinary basics while your herds thrived like nobody's business. Try *that* on the Great Plains! And life was that simple at first, but as herds grew and grazing pressure increased, some rather sizable flaws emerged with the business model.

First, there wasn't as much grazing to be had as it may have seemed. A lack of grass quickly became a serious limiting factor, and the island's steep

Left: While relatively short-lived, the mining era on Catalina is an important part of its culture, serving as a key economic model on the island until the ore played out. *Courtesy of University of Southern California Digital Library.*

Below: Ranching on Catalina also had its day in the sun, but the island's habitats proved unsuitable for sustained grazing. *Courtesy of Catalina Island Conservancy.*

In an effort to increase forage, hayfields like this one at Middle Ranch were created. Remnants of these fields are still highly visible today. *Courtesy Catalina Island Conservancy.*

topography didn't lend itself to the creation of new pastures. That didn't stop folks from trying though. Middle Ranch, which as the name implies was a major ranch located in the geographic center of the island, was the focus of serious efforts to make grazing viable, as was El Rancho Escondido several miles to the northwest. Fields were plowed and seeded with various grasses, harvested yearly for hay and managed with heavy machinery. Remnants of those fields are still visible today. Unfortunately for ranchers, the development of Middle Ranch and El Rancho Escondido couldn't add enough grazing lands to sustain the foraging situation.

Given the fact that over twenty thousand sheep were likely on the island at one time, habitat may not have seemed all that limiting in those early days. Twenty thousand is an impressive number, but at those levels, the sheep were a pretty miserable lot, and the habitat they left in their wake was by all measures a complete mess. The sheep had literally eaten themselves out of house and home in less than two decades, and the island's ecosystem buckled under the pressure. The grasslands and other habitats had literally been mowed to the nubs, and whatever brave bit of greenery made an attempt to sprout would have been immediately nipped back down to the ground. Erosion began to increase, wool production tanked and whatever meat might have hung on the bones of these very hungry animals wouldn't have been very appealing or marketable. Ecologically and economically, the system crashed. And sheep weren't the only grazers roaming the land. At roughly the same time, cattle ranching was also in full swing, and the rapidly deteriorating condition of Catalina's habitats took their toll here as well. And then there were the goats, which consumed almost everything the other grazers didn't get to. Later came the pigs, which added insult to injury by rooting up the ground and killing plants outright. Catalina was being grazed far beyond its carrying capacity.

Once an ecological system has been hammered to the point of collapse, it doesn't spring back to high health as soon as you relieve the grazing pressure. Scaling back the herds might have helped a bit, but it would've taken time for recovery, and time is money. The ranchers simply could no longer afford to ranch. If you want a sense of how far out of whack the situation was, consider this: the Catalina Island Conservancy conducted studies in the 1990s to determine the maximum number of bison, another introduced species, that Catalina could sustainably support in a healthy condition, and the answer was 150. It turns out that the notion of intensive grazing over the long haul was, let's just say, optimistic. Grazing as a serious economic effort had all but collapsed by the 1950s, leaving only place names like "Middle

Sheep grazing during the early 1900s. Note the condition of the land, with little browse remaining and erosion beginning to impact the landscape. *Courtesy of University of Southern California Digital Library.*

Goats once roamed Catalina. The condition of the landscape in this image gives one a sense of the limited capacity for sustained grazing. *Courtesy of University of Southern California Digital Library.*

Ranch," "El Rancho Escondido," "Sheep Chute" and "Skull Canyon" to remind us of Catalina's brief ranching era.

With miners, ranchers, adventurers and various others beginning to flow more easily back and forth from the mainland, word of Catalina's unique and rugged beauty began to spread. By no small coincidence, the Catalina buzz began humming at about the same time that westerners were creating a rather interesting concept—leisure time. Tourism was about to become a thing, and those who saw it coming decided that owning land might be a wise investment.

Over the years, a number of individuals laid claim to various parts of Catalina, but the first to actually buy the entire island was George Lick, who managed to get control of Catalina in its entirety in 1867. Lick sold the island to a gentleman by the name of George Shatto for $200,000 in 1887. Lick was a fascinating man who was involved in everything from the founding of Ghirardelli Chocolates in San Francisco to the creation of the Lick Observatory in 1888, home to the largest refracting telescope in the world at the time. He was also, for a long while, the richest man in California.

George Shatto stands out as the first entrepreneur to purchase the island with a strong vision for transforming it into a world-class tourism destination. He got right to work drawing up plans for safe harbor and a town in what the Tongva called the Bay of Seven Moons. His sister-in-law Etta Whitney came up with the name Avalon, in reference to an island in King Arthur's day. Shatto succeeded in building the Hotel Metropole and managed to get a wharf in working shape for his steamer, the *Ferndale*—but not without a few fits and starts. Shatto learned what others had learned before him: owning and running an island can be a pricey, risky and uncertain affair. George's money gave out long before his balance sheets turned positive.

Shatto managed to hang on until 1892 before he went bankrupt. At that time, Catalina briefly returned to the Lick estate. But the idea of a tourist destination resonated with a lot of people, none more at the time than the Banning family. Phineas Banning had been running ships to the island throughout the Shatto years. In fact, a few years before Shatto even bought the place, the Banning family had established the Wilmington Transportation Company and began shuttling people to and from Catalina. When Shatto fell into debt in 1892, the Bannings saw their opportunity. They bought the island from the Lick estate and immediately added more ships to the schedule, making Catalina a bona fide tourist stop.

It should be noted that the Bannings also needed rock to build a breakwater at their Wilmington location, and Catalina had an outstanding quarry location that is still in operation today. In any event, tourism was key to the investment, and if it was going to work, there was much to be done. The Bannings got busy. They provided running water and electricity, worked out the basics of waste disposal, built the first real roads and even got some social services in place, including police and fire protection. But that stuff was all just a framework for tourism. People didn't shell out good money to come and check out the fire department—they wanted fun things to do! The Bannings handled that too. They created a Greek amphitheater, which although run down still stands today just above the people's park or what the locals call "Machine Gun Park" due to the World War II–era machine gun mounted there. If you visit Catalina, it's worth a stroll up the hill just past the park to visit the ruins. The Bannings also built what's reported to be one of the first golf courses on the West Coast, as well as a dance pavilion, tennis courts, a small aquarium and even an elevated lift that would scoot you from the amphitheater up to a great viewing area on the ridge. The cement pilings for the lift are still visible up near the Inn at Mt. Ada, and the view alone makes the site worth a visit. Given that the Bannings were stagecoach innovators, there had to be stagecoach rides. They even created what appear to be the world's first glass-bottomed boats. They clearly had it together. Things went well for the Bannings until 1915, when a catastrophic fire burned half of Avalon's buildings to the ground.

But the Bannings liked Catalina and decided to press on. They doubled down and began creating the Saint Catherine's Hotel. The hotel was to be located on Sugarloaf Point (where the casino building stands today), which would have been pretty spectacular, but construction costs, including the work of blowing up and hauling away Sugarloaf rock itself, proved too expensive. They built Saint Catherine's on Descanso Beach instead, a short distance from Avalon. But history seemed to be conspiring against the Bannings. Not only were they squeezed financially from fires and cost overruns, but in 1914, World War I broke out, putting the brakes on the tourist trade. Catalina and its entire infrastructure were sold in shares in 1919. It had been a wild twenty-seven years, and the Bannings had made a lasting mark. They had almost singlehandedly presided over the most significant transformation of Catalina as they ushered the island into the modern age.

Among a handful of additional early investors was William Wrigley Jr. After he first experienced the island, he was determined to buy out all of the other shareholders, and before the year was out, he held a controlling interest in the Santa Catalina Island Company. Wrigley knew that the Bannings had been on the right track, and with deep pockets, a quick mind and excellent business

Historic photo of Avalon after a fire in 1915 devastated the town. *Courtesy of* Catalina Islander.

sense, Wrigley set about promoting and building a Catalina that would finally become a world-class tourist destination. He set out to make sure people far and wide understood that there was "No Trip Like It in the World."

Wrigley poured millions of dollars into his vision. He added the SS *Avalon* and the SS *Catalina* to the fleet in order to bring more visitors to the island in style. Where Sugarloaf once stood, he created a dance hall the likes of which had never been seen. He called it the Casino, long before Las Vegas developers started using the term. Gambling never took place in the Avalon Casino, but the venue did serve as a focal point during the Big Band era. Anyone who was anyone in the heyday of swing played the Casino, with its incredible custom-built dance floor and massive vaulted ceilings. Many of the attractions from this era are either still functioning (like the Casino) or still standing in various states of disrepair. Such is this case with Bird Park, the Chimes Tower and even Descanso Beach, though the latter has now been redesigned as a modern beachfront getaway. Wrigley even brought his baseball team, the Chicago Cubs, to Avalon for their spring trainings. The ball field they played on, called the "Field of Dreams," is much reduced

William Wrigley Jr. on the streets of Avalon, circa 1919. *Courtesy of Catalina Island Museum.*

today but can still be found behind Avalon's current city hall. In any event, tourism boomed in the Wrigley era, and there was to be no turning back.

It was during this time that Catalina really came of age as a tourist destination. As you'll see, tourism on the island is still driven by the vision of the Wrigleys and their predecessors. But the town of Avalon occupies just the tiniest portion of Catalina Island, and the island's wild areas held an appeal as well. The Wrigleys knew that tourism was doing well, but it wasn't paying all the bills. Another model that could help the bottom line and diversify the visitor experience was needed. Enter the concept of Catalina as a sport-hunting paradise. If sportsmen were paying tidy sums for high-quality hunts from Texas to Africa, it stood to reason they might do the same on Catalina. With over forty-four thousand acres of wildlands right outside Avalon's city limits, the concept of introducing exotic animals for big-game hunting seemed like a great idea at the time. Unlike most of Wrigley's ideas, this one turned out to be, let's just say, less than ideal.

While all of this activity was underway, mining took off once again on Catalina. From approximately 1923 to 1927, zinc and silver mining had its day in the sun. It was a profitable venture for a time. The main operation ran out of White's Landing and at its peak included an aerial tramway for hauling ore from the mines uphill at Blackjack to the mill and barges below. If you know where to look, you can still find pilings and timbers from the old tramway from Blackjack all the way down to White's Landing. But when ore prices crashed in 1927, the mining operation shut down, and that was the end of serious mining on Catalina. From an ecological perspective, it's fortunate that mining never really took off on a larger industrial scale. Unlike many early mining boomtowns, Catalina is blessed in that it's spared a legacy of arsenic or massive slag heaps leaching very bad things into its precious groundwater, streams and near-shore environment. The only surviving mining operation can be found on Catalina's East End, where a large rock quarry still extracts materials for road repairs and for export to the mainland.

From 1927 until 1937, pottery and tile were made on the island at the Catalina Clay Products Company. You can find outstanding examples of these tiles across Catalina today, with perhaps the best example of the tiles found in and on the Wrigley Memorial at the Wrigley Memorial and Botanic Garden high up in Avalon Canyon. Original tiles are now highly sought-after collectibles. With the exception of some local artists producing some outstanding modern tile work, the industry as a major economic driver for the community also ran its course and faded into the past like other economic models before it.

Pigs from feral domestic stock found on Santa Rosa Island were introduced to Catalina in the 1930s. It's likely that they were brought to Catalina for sport hunting, though it's also said that they were brought here under the erroneous assumption that they would control the rattlesnake population by eating their eggs. Pigs may have trampled the occasional snake, and they certainly degraded habitats needed by snakes, but we can be sure they ate

White's Landing during the mining days. Note the structure at the lower right, where ore was received via an elevated tram from the Black Jack Mine. *Courtesy of Santa Catalina Island Company.*

precisely zero rattlesnake eggs because of one bit of scientific info: Catalina's rattlesnakes give live birth. There were no eggs to eat! In any event, pigs were introduced and quickly began to multiply. The thing about pigs is that they breed like rabbits. It's possible for a sow to have fourteen young per litter and two litters per year. That's a ridiculously high reproductive rate. In what seemed like no time at all, the pigs were eating pretty much all that was left to eat on Catalina. That meant that any native species reliant on any kind of foliage or bulbs for their survival suffered mightily.

To make things even more dramatic, the pigs weren't the only modern non-native grazers on the island. Deer were brought over from the mainland at about the same time and were going through extreme boom-and-bust cycles of their own. If you look at images from the 1930s to the late 1980s, it looks like somebody took a weed whacker to the entire island. With the addition of bison brought over in the 1920s, you could have almost heard the island's habitats groan under the strain. Individually, each of these non-native grazers presented a problem. Collectively, they represented an ecological catastrophe. Estimates made in the late 1970s showed that the island's wildlands were being overgrazed by more than 1,200 percent!

Sure the ecology was being hammered, but at least folks were making a buck, right? Actually, this was not the case. The simple fact is that Catalina is one seriously rugged place, and animals like deer and pigs know how to hide. The idea of combining hunting with tourism on Catalina never panned out over the long haul, and economically, the venture failed. The only surviving hunting operation today is carried out by the Catalina Island Conservancy through licensed hunting operators and conservancy staff. The California Department of Fish and Game tightly regulates deer hunting, and that helps a bit to reduce the impact of deer on the recovering native vegetation. Mule deer remain a challenge to the wildland managers of the conservancy, who, as we'll see in the next chapter, continue to develop strategies to manage introduced species.

Now let's review the major economic models that have been attempted to date. The gold rush failed and isn't coming back. Ranching failed and isn't coming back either. Large-scale tile and clay production had its day.

The Wrigley Memorial is located in Avalon Canyon. Note the classic Catalina tile designs on the structure. *Courtesy of Terri Bassett.*

The barren hills of Catalina, circa 1950s. This photo shows Bulrush Canyon after being grazed to an unsustainably high level. *Courtesy of University of Southern California Digital Library.*

Mining on Catalina has literally played out and isn't coming back. Tourism worked to a point but needed something else in order to generate year-round income. With the exception of tourism, all of the other models have been eliminated. The island needed something to attract visitors year-round, and that something was proving elusive.

The economics of this were not lost on William Wrigley, and it gradually dawned on him that the natural beauty of Catalina was one of its greatest assets. It was one of the things about the island that the Wrigleys treasured most—the thing that made Catalina, Catalina. The "something" that could be paired with tourism, it turned out, was nature. While they couldn't have known it at the time, the Wrigleys had set the stage for Catalina as an ecotourism destination. When we reflect on all of the economic models that have come and gone from Catalina, there's one thing that jumps out. This "new" concept of leveraging the ecological values of the land so that a healthy ecology could reinforce a healthy economy is present in only one economic model from Catalina's history, and that model belonged to the Tongva. Their economy was their ecology; they relied on it almost exclusively.

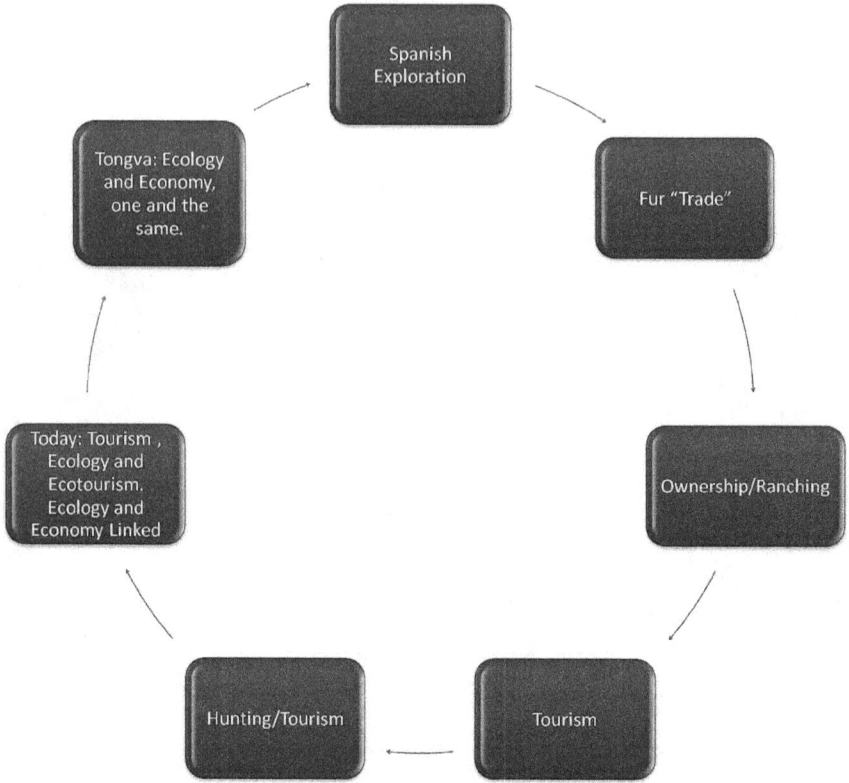

This diagram shows the economic models on Catalina over time. Note that the current model of pairing a healthy ecology with a healthy economy is also the most sustainable model ever attempted. The Tongva's economy was absolutely defined by the health of their ecology—a lesson from which Catalina has learned. *Courtesy of Frank J. Hein.*

If they lost their habitat, they would lose their livelihood. While modern societies can never live as close to the land or as in sync with their ecologies as the Tongva, we can find some wisdom in it. The "healthy ecology equals healthy economy" model has another thing going for it. The last time it was tried, it lasted for nine thousand to twelve thousand years. Unlike all other models, this one is sustainable!

Chapter 8
FULL CIRCLE

A Healthy Ecology As a Key to a Healthy Economy

In 1972, members of the Wrigley and Offield families established the Catalina Island Conservancy as an independent 501(c)(3) nonprofit organization dedicated to the conservation and preservation of Catalina Island. This bold step gave 88 percent of the island to the newly minted conservancy and ensured that specialists in the field of ecology, wildlife and habitat conservation could begin taking steps to heal an island that was ecologically wounded. But it was more than just wounded; the island's ecology was falling apart. The Wrigleys understood that conservation was a specialty field outside of their wheelhouse. Even in the early 1970s, island conservation and restoration wasn't terribly well understood by most scientists. This was the stuff of specialists, and now conservancy specialists would be taking on the job.

Clearly it was the Wrigleys' strong nature ethic that guided this bold move. They wanted to ensure that the place they loved could hold together ecologically and that by protecting the lands they could create a higher quality island experience for visitors. Keep in mind that the Wrigley's certainly could have chosen to sell off the island's wilderness in lots to subdivide it for a massive profit. Most businessmen at the time wouldn't have thought twice about it. Come to think of it, most businessmen even today wouldn't think twice about it. But instead, the Wrigleys' chose to give away the land in a way that ensured its protection and, ultimately, its restoration. In the process, they chose to walk away from millions of dollars of potential profits to do what they felt was right for the island. The world could use more of that kind of thinking today.

WHAT IS VERSUS WHAT MIGHT HAVE BEEN

Imagine if the Wrigleys had taken a different approach. What would have happened? It is easy to imagine the development of homes, condos and tourist facilities in some of the most precious beach areas of the island. Places such as Little Harbor, Shark Harbor, Middle Ranch and others would have sold to the highest bidder and been developed for maximum return on investment. Roads across the island could have been paved, which would have allowed the construction and development of urban centers across the landscape. The resident population of the island could have increased from the actual 3,500 or so residents today to perhaps tens of thousands spread across the landscape. Demands for precious fresh water, a scarce resource on such a dry island, could have increased dramatically together with a whole suite of issues dealing with human waste, energy consumption and pollution. In the process, Catalina's ecosystems would never have had the opportunity to recover, and its ecological values could have been lost here as they have been elsewhere.

So, as you plan to hike, explore or tour Catalina's wild and scenic areas, take a moment to pause, reflect and appreciate the fact that Catalina's natural values were understood and protected by those who chose not to opt for a quick buck but for a long-term vision. It's a beautiful idea. And to make that idea a reality, the powers that be set limits to infrastructure growth. Areas developed for tourism and residential uses were designed for high density and covered a minimal amount of land. This ensured that visitors would always be in close proximity to nature, able to explore and enjoy it with relative ease.

Many modern strategies in resource conservation are now present on the island: water conservation, a desalination plant, a strong recycling program, solar power sources, strict limits to the import and circulation of motor vehicles and more. There's certainly room for improvement—perhaps adding more solar power sources and creating strong incentives for electric vehicles—but the system is set up to make these things achievable. It's a start.

By creating the conservancy, the Wrigleys also solved at least two problems at once. First, they created an organization of ecologists and land managers that could begin the process of reversing centuries of serious ecological impacts. This meant that Catalina could begin pulling out of an ecological nosedive and begin to heal. Second, the vast majority of the island, which was never going to turn a profit, was now in the hands of a non-profit conservation entity. In fact, the wildlands of Catalina must have been something of a money pit for the Wrigleys. By keeping the 12 percent of the island that could clearly generate income and shifting the remainder into the hands of an organization uniquely qualified to manage it, the net profit for the Wrigleys would have improved rather dramatically. It was a win-win situation if ever there was one. The choice to form the Catalina Island Conservancy was altruistic, forward thinking and an outstanding investment in Catalina's future, but it was also a really smart business move. Owning and managing the entire island had bankrupted George Shatto, and it nearly got the Banning brothers as well. The Wrigleys had found a way to ensure that Catalina could remain economically viable and ecologically sound by understanding, as the Tongva did, that the two things are inextricably linked.

THE CATALINA ISLAND CONSERVANCY COMES OF AGE

Imagine a newly minted conservancy suddenly finding itself responsible for the ecological health of over forty-two thousand acres of land. Never mind the fact that the land is located on an island in the Pacific that's been ecologically battered for hundreds of years. There was a lot of infrastructure work to be done. There were roads to manage, buildings to care for, public needs to accommodate, as well as camps and coves spread across the shores and natural resource issues galore.

The conservancy clearly had its work cut out. The first thing to do would be to take stock of the island and figure out exactly what had been inherited and what condition it was in. Until they understood what they had, they wouldn't be able to manage it. Of course, this involved a lot more than just strolling across the property and taking in the scenery. There were wildlife and habitat surveys to be done, roads to be graded, fences to be either fixed or removed, plants and bugs to inventory and a plan to put together. Given the scale of the job, the complicated logistics of getting around the island and its ecological condition, it took over a decade to complete the baseline work needed to understand what Wild Catalina was all about.

As biologists systematically surveyed plants, birds, mammals, mice, reptiles and more, it became clear that Catalina was special—an ecological jewel just waiting to be restored. But Catalina also had its problems, some small and some very big. Bringing Catalina back to ecological health was going to be a challenging job. What kinds of issues did they face? Let's see—non-

Above: Researchers on Catalina examine the health of an island stream. *Courtesy of Alexis Romero*.

Left: The flax-leaved broom is one of the more persistent invasive plants to have taken root on Catalina. It is a threat to the island's ecological health. *Courtesy of Carlos de la Rosa*.

native bison, an overpopulation of deer, non-native and overpopulated goats and pig populations literally rooting Catalina's plant ecology into oblivion. Plants? Hundreds of species of non-natives and invasives as far as the eye could see. Habitat? Hammered. Doing everything at once would take more resources than anyone could muster.

On the one hand, the conservancy had to start taking care of immediate needs like road grading, property management and partnership development. On the other hand, its primary focus had to be on long-term conservation. If they were going to get the island's ecology right, they had to get the habitats right. While that sounds nice and neat, there's the complicating factor in nature that everything is connected. There was no single factor putting a hurt on Wild Catalina; there were dozens, all intertwined. But which was the biggest threat? You could remove invasive plants and put native foliage into the ground, but the pigs, deer, bison and goats would simply mow them down or root them up. It would be a waste of time and money. Managing all the non-natives at once was too labor intensive and expensive. You could put up fences to try and keep things out, but deer would jump over, and bison just plow through them. The answers weren't obvious. All solutions were labor and cash intensive, and this clearly was not going to be easy.

INTRODUCED ANIMALS ON CATALINA

Over many decades, as we related in previous chapters, a number of non-native species were introduced to the island for various purposes. Here's a quick breakdown.

Feral pigs: Introduced in 1934 as biological agents for rattlesnakes and/or sport-hunting programs, the animals came from Santa Rosa Island, where they had been introduced in the 1800s. As many as twelve thousand feral pigs were removed from Catalina from 1990 to 2003. It is believed that there is still one remaining pig that has avoided capture.

Goats: Domestic goats that eventually became feral were introduced to Catalina during the 1830s. At one point, there were as many as fifteen thousand roaming freely across the island. There are no more than three remaining sterile individuals on the island, all confined to small areas in the West End.

Cattle: Introduced as a business in the late 1800s, all cattle were eventually removed from the island by 1954 as the business ceased to become profitable.

Bison: Fourteen bison were brought to Catalina in 1924 for the filming of the silent movie *The Vanishing American*. The animals were released into the wildlands after the filming was completed. Several more were brought to the island with the purpose of maintaining a breeding population, which at one point reached over six hundred.

Mule Deer: Introduced along with white-tailed deer (which never became established) in the 1930s for sport-hunting programs, mule deer are still roaming free on Catalina, including a semi-urban population that lives in Avalon Canyon. These deer are owned by the State of California and are managed by a sports-hunting program regulated by the California Department of Fish and Game.

Blackbuck Antelope: A few individuals of this Asian species were introduced in 1972 as an attempt to establish a big-game preserve on Catalina. Only a few antelope persist to this day, mostly confined to the upper parts of Sweetwater Canyon below the Airport in the Sky.

Feral Cats: We really don't know exactly when domestic cats were introduced to the island, but many of them eventually became feral. Today, they roam the interior of the island doing what cats do best: hunting. Evidence exists that the feral cat population was well established in the 1930s. A recent survey of cat colonies (groups of feral cats that receive food and water from people) estimated the number of feral cats on the island at over one thousand.

Rodents (e.g. black rats, Norway rats and house mice): These species were most likely introduced by boat, perhaps as early as the arrival of the first European ships. They compete with a number of native and endemic rodents.

Other Species: These include wild turkeys, European starlings, house sparrows, rock doves (also known as the common pigeon), spotted doves, bullfrogs, at least one species of turtle, wide-mouth bass, perch and sheep. Of these, the starlings, doves, turtles, bullfrogs and fish are still present on the island.

It became clear that until the conservancy got the heavy overgrazing under control, habitat improvements were all but certain to be immediately eaten away by hungry, non-native browsers. Removing the most damaging of the grazers would need to be an early step. A couple of things fell in the conservancy's favor. For one thing, the sheep and cattle days had already run their course. With no money to be made and no market for ranching on Catalina, cattle and sheep had simply ebbed away on their own by around

One of several non-native animals introduced to the island, the mule deer is one of the more voracious omnivores on Catalina. Even Avalon isn't off limits. *Courtesy of Julie King.*

1950. That left bison, pigs, goats and deer on the list. Bison, it turns out would be the easiest of the wild species to manage. They stick together, wander around in large herds and, for the most part, spend their time in open, easy-to-access grassy areas. Goats and pigs, however, were a very different story. First of all, there were a whole lot more of them than bison, and they reproduced a whole lot faster. Second of all, these animals do not stick together in easy-to-reach locations like bison do. They're everywhere, and they know how to hide. Deer presented a special complication—the Catalina Island Conservancy didn't have authority over their fate. If you wanted to manage the deer, you had to go through the State of California's process. So, deer were not under the conservancy's direct control, which made their management a bit tricky and perhaps not the best first choice. Bison were an excellent place to start.

Bison also presented one of the first really interesting philosophical quandaries for the conservancy. The animals were non-native, clearly impacting habitats and in the 1970s were overpopulated. The conservancy had every right to simply herd them up and cull them, but that's not what it did. The action it took sheds light on the rather unusual balancing act the organization finds itself in to this day.

When the conservancy was formed, there were more than 600 bison on Catalina, and they were not in good shape. There was only so much grass to go around on Catalina, and it was clear that there was nowhere near enough to keep this number healthy. From a pure conservation standpoint, the easy answer was to just remove them from the island. But remember that the conservancy's mission includes conservation, education and recreation, and bison were one of the most sought-after animals to view by visitors. Catalina's community and its economy would feel the loss if bison were to suddenly disappear, and that mattered to the conservancy, which began wondering if there

Non-native but managed to minimize impact, bison are an example of an intelligent balance of resource and human desires. *Courtesy of Frank J. Hein.*

might be a "magic number" of bison that could be manageable without a significant ecological impact. It decided to take a closer look. What it found was essentially this: bison are grass eaters, and most of the grasses by on the island were non-native. Studies showed that there was enough grass on the island to keep about 150 bison in good condition. A plan gradually emerged to manage the herds, keep the numbers in the sweet spot and

Managing bison in the past meant rounding them up for eventual repatriation on the Rosebud Sioux Indian Reservation in South Dakota. *Courtesy of Catalina Island Conservancy.*

ensure that enough (but not too many) bison roamed the island and could be seen by visitors. Would Catalina's habitats be better off without bison? Likely, but because bison are manageable, the impact could be controlled, and it was a price the conservancy was willing to pay.

At first, to reach this number, bison were routinely rounded up and shipped to market on the mainland. That was fine, except for the fact that many of the animals were essentially being sent to slaughter, and in California, more so than in other places, that had its issues. In 2005, an amazing partnership was forged between the Catalina Island Conservancy and the Morongo Band of Indians. The plan was to round up Catalina's extra bison and, instead of shipping them to market, ship them to a place where they were native and where they were wanted and needed. One of those places was the Rosebud Indian Reservation in South Dakota. The repatriation of bison to their native lands was a great idea, a terrific partnership and an emotionally moving action.

While an outstanding project for a time, it too had its issues. It cost roughly $1,000 per animal to ship out, and all the handling and moving was tough on the animals. From the conservancy's standpoint, the problem was that

In an adaptive approach to bison management, darting each female bison in the herd with a safe and effective contraceptive is proving to be ideal. *Courtesy of Calvin Duncan.*

this model also forced it to wait until bison numbers climbed to well over the recommended 150 before they could be rounded up and shipped out. That meant that the island still had more bison than it could handle.

In 2009, conservancy biologists adapted their approach when they tested a relatively new contraceptive called Porcine Zona Pellucida, or PZP. The idea was that if you could dart every female in the herd with a dose of the contraceptive, most wouldn't get pregnant, and you could control the herd with more precision. The contraceptive was originally developed for human use, so it was safe, but it was found to be only 95 percent effective, which is a bit less than perfect for humans. But that rate was perfect for bison, as old age, injury and disease would balance things out. Long story short, it appears to be working. This new approach is relatively easy and inexpensive to administer, and the population can be held to the ideal number with only minor population swings. Since the implementation of the program, bison herd numbers have held steady at or very near the target rate of 150. Relatively speaking, that was pretty easy. If only all wildlife management could go this smoothly!

Feral Pigs and Goats

One of the most controversial but effective conservation actions that the Catalina Island Conservancy undertook in the 1990s and early 2000s involved the removal of thousands of feral pigs and goats from the island. It has been widely documented around the world that the introduction of exotic herbivores, especially to island ecosystems, can dramatically degrade the composition, abundance and distribution of native flora and fauna, leading to numerous extinctions. Throughout history, humans have introduced non-native species to island environments both intentionally and accidentally. Among the most frequently introduced species are domestic food animals. If allowed to range freely, livestock will gradually begin to resemble their wild ancestors, and after several generations, many species become feral. Currently, feral animals are of great concern to many land managers in protected areas. Feral and exotic animal control and removal is a recurring topic for the federal agencies and private organizations responsible for managing the California Channel Islands. In January 1990, the conservancy began a habitat and ecological restoration project designed to mitigate decades of degradation caused by large populations of feral goats (*Capra hircus*) and feral pigs (*Sus scrofa*) on Catalina Island.

The conservancy sought an economically viable long-term plan to protect the native communities of the island. Several options to address feral animals were considered, including sustained management, live capture and removal, biochemical sterilization, introduction of predators and eradication. After a cost and feasibility analysis, the conservancy's board of directors agreed that all the animals should be removed through lethal methods in the most humane manner possible. The analysis revealed that sustained management would not completely or reliably alleviate the environmental damage caused by feral herbivores and noted that live capture and removal has caused stress and high mortality rates in other studies. The cost of large-scale removal was logistically impractical and highly prohibitive. It also found that biochemical birth control had not been proven effective and that application to the entire population (or all of one sex of either species) was also cost-prohibitive and logistically impossible. Finally, the analysis cited numerous examples in which the use of introduced predators to control non-native animals was ineffective. This ran counter to the goals of the conservancy, as introduced predators would not limit their activities to the consumption of exotic herbivores, could negatively impact native fauna and would themselves eventually need to be removed.

In 1990, the Institute for Wildlife Studies (IWS) was contracted to begin feral goat removal efforts on the west end of Catalina Island. The success of that initial program resulted in an island-wide feral goat eradication plan beginning in 1992. In conjunction with the feral goat removal, a formalized program was initiated to control feral pigs. Since 1990, approximately 8,200 goats have been removed from the island. This includes the limited use of non-lethal methods in 2000 and 2001.

In 1996, a feral pig removal pilot study was conducted by IWS on the island's west end as well. The apparent recovery of several native plant species, such as tree poppy (*Dendromecon rigida rhamnoides*), following their removal illustrated the benefits of a removal program compared to previous control efforts. In July 1998, the conservancy contracted IWS to expand the feral animal removal (FAR) program across the entire island. The overall goals of the FAR program involved a six-year plan to remove all feral goats and pigs from Catalina Island. To facilitate this plan, the island was divided into four zones, and fences were constructed to prevent animals from moving between zones. The California Department of Fish and Game issued a "Memorandum of Understanding" that allowed IWS to pursue feral pigs using alternatives to approved methodologies for public hunting, and these alternative techniques were proven effective in the eradication effort.

Chapter 9
A UNIQUE PLACE AND AN INNOVATIVE MODEL

THE WRIGLEYS SET A BALANCE IN MOTION

In order to fully understand how the Catalina of yesteryear became the Catalina of today, we need to go back just a bit to add some detail to the Wrigley story. The year was 1919. Mr. William Wrigley Jr. was already an incredibly successful businessman, with the William Wrigley Jr. Company bringing innovations to the market. His famous offer of two packages of chewing gum for each purchase of a can of baking powder revolutionized the business world, albeit not exactly as planned. When the Wrigley Company realized that people were buying the baking powder strictly to get the gum, they took the hint and ultimately made Wrigley's Spearmint gum America's favorite chewing gum.

With his wealth increasing, Mr. Wrigley purchased the Chicago Cubs baseball team and a mansion in Pasadena. Then a fateful event occurred. While looking at postcards of Catalina during a conversation with a real estate broker, William Wrigley Jr. decided to purchase the "island in the Pacific" that was for sale by the Banning Brothers. Upon visiting the island with his wife, Ada Elizabeth, the couple fell in love with "the mountain," as he called it. He decided, apparently on the spot, that the island was calling to him, and he was determined to purchase it.

William's concept for developing Catalina made it necessary to purchase all rights from the early partners, which he managed to do.

Mr. Wrigley did not want a "Coney Island flavor" on Catalina, but rather to preserve the beauty of the island's natural setting. His idea was to make it a better resort and "available to the people to whom I owe my prosperity."

His approach included the construction of hotels in Avalon (1919) and the Wrigley Mansion at Mt. Ada (1920), an undersea cable to connect the island telephonically to the mainland (1923) and the creation of the Thompson Dam and Reservoir in Middle Canyon, which was needed to provide fresh water to the growing town. Wrigley donated land for a school and opened the colorful Bird Park and the now iconic Catalina Island Casino. These projects increased visitation to the island from some 90,000 people in 1919 to 750,000 in 1929. It was a stunning achievement, and now Catalina was literally swinging. All the popular acts of the Big Band era came to play at the casino, and they drew thousands of people each night. There were evenings during which 5,000 or more people filled the casino for epic nights of music and dancing.

Upon William Wrigley Jr.'s death in 1932, his son Phillip K. Wrigley took over the business of running the island. He continued the development path set by his father by improving the infrastructure and available amenities. But through all of these developments, Wrigley's awareness and ethics held the island's beauty intact. After all, it was the island's beauty that had attracted the Wrigley family in the first place, and it was the island's beauty that made it such a special place for both islanders and tourists. Even in the 1920s, access to unspoiled natural beauty was getting hard to come by, and the Wrigleys understood that the natural beauty of the island was a major factor in its appeal. It was this deeply held belief that shaped perhaps the most important decision in Catalina's modern history—what to do with the rest of the island!

It was one thing to hold this idea philosophically and quite another to put it in motion. By the late 1960s, as the concept of an ecologically sound Catalina was incubating, the island's wildlands were getting less beautiful by the minute, with soils eroding, plants being decimated and more. Something bold needed to be done to turn things around. That "something" the Wrigleys came up with was a doozy, and as doozies go, this one was decades ahead of its time.

The History of the Conservancy: From Humble Beginnings to a Full-Fledged Conservation Machine

By the early 1970s, the Wrigley family had owned Catalina Island for more than fifty years. During that time, they became interested in conserving the natural beauty and wildlife of the island and in 1972 established the Catalina Island Conservancy. With this gift, 88 percent of Catalina Island and over fifty miles of its coastline were given permanent status as a wildlands preserve. In 1974, the Santa Catalina Island Company entered a fifty-year open space agreement with Los Angeles County that guaranteed "public recreational and educational use of 41,000 acres of Santa Catalina Island, consistent with good land conservation practices." Then, on February 15, 1975, the Santa Catalina Island Company (representing the interests of the Wrigley and Offield families) deeded 42,135 acres to the new non-profit organization, including the 41,000-acre easement.

When the conservancy was formed, much of Southern California's coastline was still relatively wild. Today, Catalina Island is one of the last remaining examples of undeveloped coastline in the region. The island offers the peace and respite usually relegated to distant lands: clean air, breathtaking vistas and unparalleled opportunities for people to connect with nature. In recent years, experts have determined that these rich, renewing experiences with nature are essential for a healthy human condition. As wild spaces decrease and the demand for access to those that remain rises, the conservancy can expect increasing pressure to meet the needs for recreation and interpretive enrichment, as well as setting the standard for conservation management and training future generations of scientists concerned with land stewardship.

The Wrigley family shared a vision of Catalina as a resort for people from all stations of life with a strong emphasis placed on conservation and protection of the natural and cultural resources. Between 1919 and 1972, various conservation practices were initiated by the Wrigley-led Santa Catalina Island Company, including much-needed animal control, watershed protection and the reseeding of overgrazed areas. As we'll see later, many plants and animals introduced during the ranching years had created many of the conservation issues that the conservancy now faces. These introduced plants and animals were decimating the native landscape of Catalina. Since then, the conservancy has been committed to the long-term management and improvement of the quality of the island's native habitats and the sustainable use of the island and its near-shore environments.

MISSION OF THE CATALINA ISLAND CONSERVANCY

"To be a responsible steward of its land through a balance of conservation, education and recreation." This is the conservancy's mission statement. Its main goals lie in the protection, restoration and management of its lands using environmental education and outdoor recreation as tools to provide sustainable and low-impact access to the public. Current activities and initiatives include:

Wildlife management
Catalina Island fox recovery
Bald eagle restoration
Bison and mule deer management
Pets and wildlife management
Land birds monitoring
Marine mammals monitoring
Plant ecology
Fire areas monitoring and protection
Rare plant database
Protection and restoration of rare habitats and species
Invasive plant management
Fire areas monitoring and management
Federal, state and other projects
Monitoring and addressing invasive species
Best management practices program
Restoration of degraded areas
Native plant nurseries
Restoration sites inventory
Watershed map
Restoration projects at Windward Beaches, landslide areas and others
Environmental education and outreach
Youth programs
Adult education and outreach
Pets and wildlife education initiatives
Operation of The Nature Center at Avalon Canyon
Recreation and Access Programs
Trans-Catalina Trail
Jeep ecotours

Biking, hiking, camping and horseback riding
Weddings and special events
Volunteer vacation and other volunteer opportunities

These efforts will remain an important focus for the conservancy into the foreseeable future. Over the next few decades, the conservancy plans to continue the restoration and improvement of the ecology of the island through modeling best conservation management practices. It also aims to make Catalina a world-class ecological destination and a leader in providing outstanding nature experiences that delight a broad audience. The conservancy aspires to build ecological literacy and influence sustainable behavior—both locally and regionally—while also lending its expertise to broader conservation and sustainable development discussions that are shaping our world.

Chapter 10
WHEN NATURE NEEDS A HAND, PART 1

Doing Good for the Land

The world is constantly changing, but in the last few hundred years or so, many of the changes caused by humans have become disconcerting. It is tempting to think of our footprint on the planet as superficial or of little importance for such a large, old planet, but humans are an incredibly successful species—one without precedent in the history of earth. Our activities have left impacts on the landscape that can be viewed even from the vastness of outer space. Our values have also changed and continue to change. The ways in which we see and use the natural resources of the planet have evolved over millennia, influencing the rise and fall of entire civilizations, the green revolution of agriculture, the accelerated development of technology and the alteration of critical natural systems such as weather and climate patterns. Humans occupy and touch just about every habitat present on earth, and we are learning that it is time for us to be more thoughtful about our impact on the planet we call home.

The modern conservation movement, based on science and guided by principles of sustainability and long-term survival, is guiding us as we begin to address the problems we currently face as a civilization. The specters of global climate change and the ongoing worldwide biodiversity crisis are enormously difficult issues to face, but they are not impossible challenges.

We humans have some hard decisions to make in the upcoming decades—decisions that will require a rethinking of our values and relationship with the natural world. When viewed in a world context, healing the landscape can seem like an impossible feat. But Catalina and the ecological successes accomplished here stand as powerful and positive reminders that when we put our minds, muscles and resources behind an effort, amazing things can happen. In this chapter, we'll explore a couple of notable cases and situations on Catalina in which a change in philosophy and approach has led to significant and lasting conservation successes. These cases represent models of thinking and acting, mergers of intellect and technology, passion, effort, commitment and even bravery against the odds. On Catalina, we are pleased to say that nature is recovering.

TREASURES FOUND AND ALMOST LOST

We'll start with the story of the Catalina Island fox. We know that this small carnivore is a descendant of similar foxes from the northern Channel Islands, which themselves descended from the gray fox (*Urocyon cinereoargenteus*), a common denizen of the American continent. The island relatives eventually became a separate species (*Urocyon littoralis*) through the process of genetic isolation from the original population, mutations and genetic drift. Small changes over thousands of years gave rise to six distinct subspecies, each on a different Channel Island, with each population genetically distinct.

We know little about the early adventures of the Catalina Island fox, mostly because we don't have records of their bones from ancient times. As noted earlier, their arrival on Catalina coincided roughly with that of the first Native American residents, the Tongva, and it is likely that the foxes were brought here by them. The earliest estimates of the fox's population, recorded in the 1970s and '80s, put the population at between 1,500 and 2,000, a relatively small number of animals. In 1999 and 2000, people started noticing a decline in sightings of foxes on the island. Biologists looked into the situation and discovered something very dire—most of the population had vanished! The population had crashed, and there were only about 100 foxes left on the entire island. This crash had happened in a single breeding season, and numbers were still dropping. Biologists quickly discovered that a particularly virulent form of canine distemper virus had spread through the population, and if something weren't done quickly, the entire subspecies would be headed for extinction.

A portrait of the endearing Catalina Island fox Tachi, who was born in captivity, bonded with humans rather than foxes and was an ambassador for her species. *Courtesy of Carlos de la Rosa.*

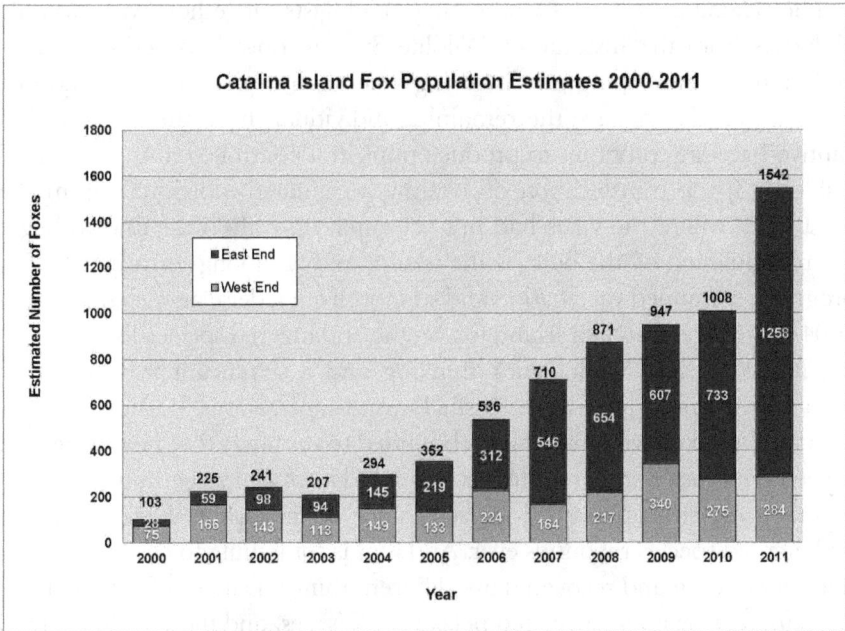

Catalina Island Fox Population Estimates 2000-2011

This chart shows the number and distribution of foxes during and after the 2000 population crash due to an outbreak of canine distemper. The 2011 records show that foxes have recovered to pre-crash numbers. *Courtesy of Calvin Duncan and Julie King.*

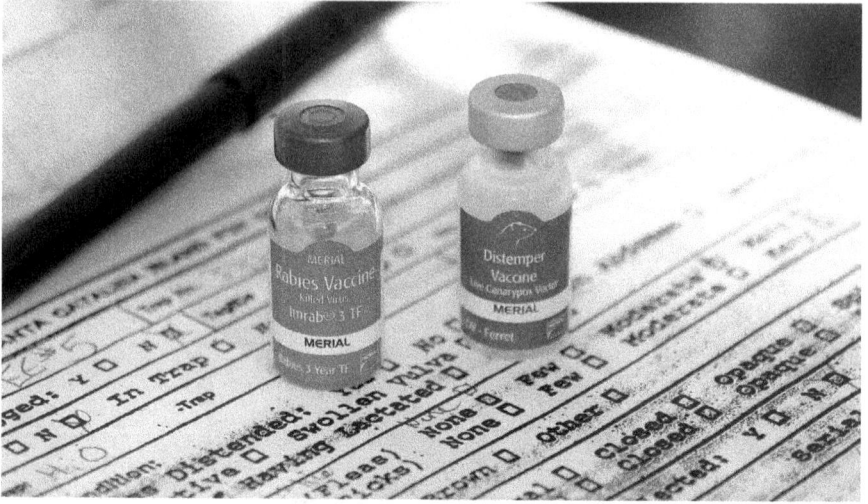

The availability of a vaccine originally intended for black-footed ferrets was a critical component of the recovery of the Catalina Island fox. *Courtesy of Carlos de la Rosa.*

The Catalina Island Conservancy biologists, together with wildlife biologists from the Institute of Wildlife Studies, dove into action with an ambitious recovery program involving several strategies: (1) acquisition of a special vaccine to save the remaining individuals from the disease; (2) a captive breeding program to produce pups in a controlled and accelerated fashion; (3) the translocation of healthy, vaccinated individuals from the West End (where the virus had not yet entered) to the East End to begin the repopulation of the bulk of the island; and (4) a long-term monitoring program, continued vaccination and support from federal agencies, which in 2004 placed the Catalina Island fox on the endangered species list.

Thanks to hard work, quick thinking and a significant investment of resources, the program was successful beyond expectations. Within a decade, the population of wild foxes had rebounded to numbers that now appear to exceed pre-crash numbers. The fox was saved from almost certain extinction in a recovery effort that is recognized as one of the fastest, if not *the* fastest, endangered species rebounds ever. And that is something to celebrate! Note that rebounding and recovered are different things. Danger of disease from feral animals or non-vaccinated pets are still issues, and the Catalina Island fox remains listed as an endangered species in spite of the population's current health.

The Channel Islands Bald Eagle

An enduring symbol of the United States, the bald eagle is a charismatic, beloved and revered species in the country. Eagles have played important roles in Native American cultures, and they play a key role in the ecology of the Channel Islands. For thousands of years, bald eagles nested on the cliffs and ridges of Catalina Island, surveying their territories and playing their role as a top predator in the island's ecosystem. For many years, eagles were hunted and poisoned while their eggs were collected and they suffered from habitat degradation. Then, a new but slowly evolving tragedy emerged. Chemical waste (most notably DDT and its metabolite, DDE) dumped into the ocean from an agrochemical plant on the Palos Verdes Peninsula began accumulating on the ocean floor between the mainland and the island. Small fish and invertebrates picked up small amounts of the chemical. Then the larger fish eating those fish and invertebrates would accumulate higher levels and so on until all the prey species that eagles depended on were laden with DDE. This led to major reproductive issues not only in bald eagles but also in osprey, pelicans and other fish-eating species. One of the observed effects of these chemicals, which were being absorbed into the eagles' tissues, was the thinning of their eggshells. The eggshells were becoming so thin that they could not sustain the weight of their parents and broke in the nests, ruining the prospects for reproductive success. For over four decades, no new eagle chicks were hatched on Catalina, and similar impacts reverberated across all of the Channel Islands and, indeed, the world.

In the 1980s, a young graduate student, David Garcelon, undertook studies to understand and solve the problem. Freshly laid eggs were collected from nests across the Channel Islands and carefully incubated in a laboratory. The resulting chicks (as well as additional chicks from other breeding facilities) were fostered back into nests or released into the wilderness as fledglings. Funds for the project were obtained from legal settlements with the Montrose Chemical plant, which provided resources that allowed the reintroduction of eagles to continue for almost twenty years. In 2006, a small subset of Catalina nests was watched closely as the adults laid, incubated and attempted to raise young without human assistance. The experiment worked, with eaglets successfully hatching. In 2007 and beyond, nests were left to operate without egg swapping, and incubation and gradually natural reproduction by eagles were becoming the norm. This set the stage for the full recovery of this important species

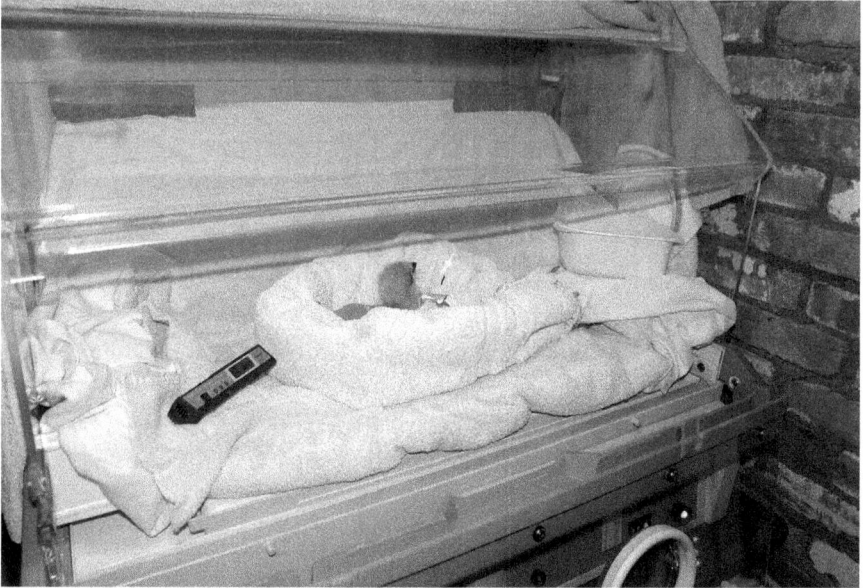

Nature occasionally needs a hand. Here a bald eagle is seen after hatching in captivity, nearly ready to be returned to its nest. *Courtesy of Carlos de la Rosa.*

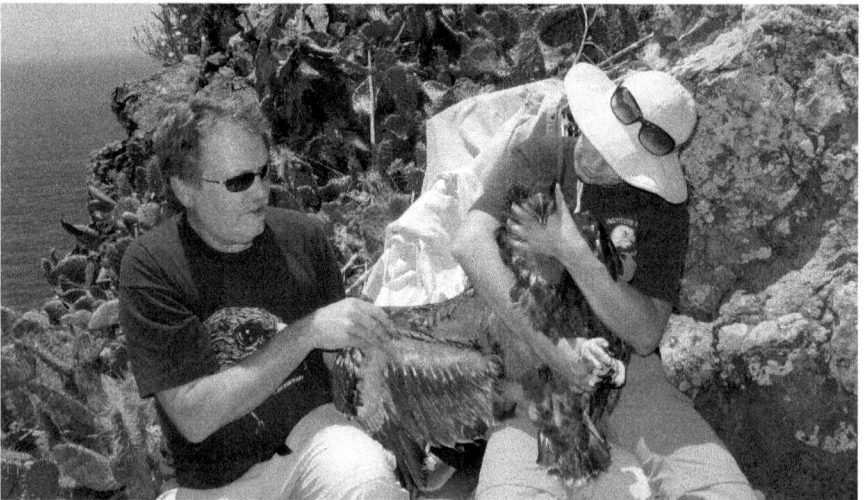

Coauthor Frank Hein and Steffani Jijón of the Institute for Wildlife Studies band eaglets in 2011. *Courtesy of Terri Bassett.*

on the Channel Islands. Contrary to popular belief, the DDT issue is not gone; rather, DDT and DDE levels have dropped just low enough in the ecosystem that, in most cases, eggs can hatch. As levels slowly continue to drop, we anticipate higher reproductive success in the future. The important thing is that the conservation efforts are a success—bald eagles are back and reproducing on their own for the first time in over fifty years!

CATALINA'S HABITATS: FIXING WHAT'S BROKEN

The stories above are just two examples of timely actions taken by dedicated biologists and institutions to save species and local populations from extinction. In these cases, disease and careless disposal of chemicals were the culprits, and decisive action on the part of the island's caretakers and collaborators avoided the tragedy of extinction. There are other successes as well, including invasive species being eliminated, species once thought extinct being rediscovered and habitat quality across all of Catalina recovering significantly. A key reason for the recovery of Catalina's habitats was the removal of non-native species such as pigs and goats, and this action is high on the list of conservation successes. But not everyone was pleased with the action. It took significant political will to accomplish, and it proved controversial among many of the island's long-term residents who had grown up hunting the animals and took issue with the species being eliminated.

Somewhere at the heart of this tension is the fact that humans have long accepted the practice of introducing species for meat or sport hunting without considering their potential impacts on the ecosystem. These introductions threatened to change forever the character of Catalina in the same way they had on hundreds of islands around the world over the centuries. In this case, however, it was the conservancy's mandate to take action and conserve the island's natural resources. Now, nearly a decade later, with the quality of the island habitat rebounding and increased ecotourism revenue being realized by island businesses, the bitterness surrounding the pig and goat eradication is subsiding. Conservation, contrary to popular belief, is not one long group hug. This stuff can be hard.

On many islands around the world, introduced non-native species are being systematically removed from the fragile island ecosystems, allowing for the comeback of the native species. Notable examples include the Galapagos

Islands, the Hawaiian Islands and New Zealand, where invasive species have caused or accelerated the extinction of many endemic species. Sometimes removing the non-native species is relatively easy, but often it is not. Some species are very hard to remove once established, while others become very adept at avoiding traps or nets or have adaptations that allow them to re-colonize easily (for example, long-living seeds that can stay viable in the soil for decades). Most of the time, removals must be done by lethal means, which, especially in California, is a recipe for conflict. On Catalina, however, meaningful conservation actions can transcend short-term conflicts and lead to long-term ecological and economic gains.

Chapter 11
WHEN NATURE NEEDS A HAND, PART 2

Elements of a Healthy Island Ecology

What is a "healthy island ecology" anyway? To answer this question, one must consider philosophical questions regarding the role of humans in the ecosystem and our ability and responsibility to implement tough changes in order to save certain species from extinction and to help Catalina recover. To this point, we've focused primarily on species eradication as a tool, but it's actually not the most common tool used by ecologists. On a broader scale, conservation organizations are often involved in restoration. We know humans have made many changes to the island. We have brought species of plants and animals from other parts of the world to the island that have outcompeted native species, and some of these arrivals will persist on Catalina for many years to come. But if we want to restore the island, at what point would you consider it restored? Should we restore it to pre-European times? That sounds eco-friendly, but it's not really a reasonable target. The city of Avalon didn't exist in pre-European times, but nobody is even remotely considering having it do anything but thrive.

One would also need to know if target conditions were even achievable. There are invasive species like flax-leaved broom, which may actually be impossible to remove. Or at best, all of the conservancy's time could be spent removing just one plant species, and that wouldn't be smart. A more realistic goal would be to restore the functional ecology of Catalina to as natural

Paradise regained. Little and Shark Harbors on the Windward side of the island are seen in their current ecological glory. *Courtesy of Carlos de la Rosa.*

a state as is reasonable, given social and economic realities. That means choices need to be made, and they need to be made with community buy-in and involvement. Such a recovery could be defined as one where native species, especially those that are found nowhere else in the world, are safe and thriving; where a balance exists between our human needs and quality, functional ecologies. The exceptional thing about this approach is that the human and ecological needs on Catalina are highly compatible. The better the ecology functions, the better island residents will fare. That can show itself via greater year-round income from an increasing eco-tourism market, or via a resilient natural system that provides ecological services to islanders simply by being healthy. There are many ways this can happen but here's a favorite. Back when the island was heavily overgrazed, tall shrubs and plants were largely absent. As marine layers move across Catalina, they deposit water on the surfaces of the plants they come in contact with. As habitats recover, the amount of surface area of plants increases exponentially and it's reasonable to expect that additional water is being captured by plants that didn't exist just a decade ago. The amount of water captured is actually very significant for an island that receives little in the way of rainfall. Stable soils are another outcome of recovered landscapes and that means that soils stay on the land during rain events, and don't wash out into the sea. Clear oceans really do come from upstream and if you run a kayaking or snorkeling operation on Catalina, clear oceans are a godsend.

The people of Catalina are inextricably linked to the island's processes and its ecology. They depend on the island to provide clean water, clean air, and landscapes worthy of touring. As stewards of the island, the conservancy is responsible for its health and its long-term viability and stability, and those things in turn, create significant value for all who live work or play on Catalina. The path that the island's community and the conservancy have embarked on is one that promises far more cooperation and mutual benefit than conflict, and that bodes well for its economic and ecological health.

Plants: New and Old

We can use the island's plant community as a starting point to explore the health of the island ecosystem. The early plant explorers that began studying the ecologies of the island encountered many species that had been brought from other places. Annual grasses, for example, had been brought early in the twentieth century to enhance the landscape for sheep and cattle operations. Many other species were brought in as ornamentals to decorate and beautify hotels and landscapes around Avalon. Pine species were brought in and planted in a number of locations, while eucalyptus trees were used extensively to stabilize soils along roads and various other locations. The reasons for doing this are varied and complex, but essentially, they filled the perceived needs of local landowners. Sometimes the impacts were not as bad as one might think, and sometimes, as in the case of flax-leaved broom, they were worse than anyone could have imagined.

Invasive Plants

Over time, some of these introduced plant species have become problematic. Eucalyptus, for example, originally from Australia, is a large family comprised of over seven hundred species, several of which were brought to the island over many years. Some eucalyptus species are considered invasive in that they take over the landscape and create adverse conditions for other plant species to live. Their fragile constitution also creates dangers from falling branches during windy days. Species like the flax-leaved broom (*Genista linifolia*) found ideal conditions in the Mediterranean-type climate of the island and established at a level that may not be reversible.

In total, over two hundred species of non-native plants have found their way here with the assistance of man. Of these, at least thirty-five are considered highly invasive and create problems to the local plant community. Invasive species share several key characteristics: they tend to be fast growing, have rapid and often prolific reproduction, have high dispersal ability, are tolerant to changing conditions, adapt rapidly to the local conditions and are able to modify their surroundings to exclude other species. When removed from their native ecosystems and placed in new areas, the natural controls—herbivores, diseases and competition—are often absent, which allows them an extraordinary advantage over the native species. They are better at taking advantage of available resources such as light, nutrients, water and space. These advantages can result in the disappearance or even extinction of local species.

So what's a conservancy to do? The Catalina Island Conservancy has developed a thoughtful and comprehensive set of strategies for dealing with invasive plants. First, they realized that not all introduced plants are invasive and that some are less likely to outcompete native species. Those considered invasive were ranked according to the magnitude of the problems they present, including how widespread they are, how fast they can spread and how damaging to the local native species they are. On the basis of this information, each highly ranked invasive species is being treated with the purpose of reducing its impact on the native communities, reducing its spread or eliminating the threat. Given their natural history, each species often requires a specific treatment, which can range from manual removal to topical chemical treatment and prevention of new introductions. All of these populations are mapped and tracked using advanced geographic information systems. This is a long process that takes many years and a sustained effort. The conservancy is committed to carry out this important work over the long haul.

MANAGING FIRE

Fire is a natural, albeit rare, phenomenon on Catalina Island. Fires caused by lightning have been recorded on the island several times, the most recent being in 2007.

Lighting strikes such as this one are rare. They are the primary source of natural fire on Catalina. *Courtesy of Carlos de la Rosa.*

After a human-caused fire, protected areas to the right of the temporary fencing survived browsing by deer. Unprotected areas did not. *Courtesy of Carlos de la Rosa.*

The natural communities on the island are adapted to fire, meaning that they can recover from a fire over time and under certain conditions. These conditions include the absence of another fire affecting the area in the near term. Most plants on the island possess adaptations for dealing with infrequent fires. For example, some plants accumulate reserves of nutrients underground in the form of "root balls" that re-sprout after a fire. Others have seeds that lie dormant in the soil and are "activated" or break dormancy after a fire. These adaptations allow for a rapid recovery.

The problem is that a great majority of fires on Catalina are *not* natural but the result of human activities. Careless campfires, improper use of tools, car fires, airplane accidents and fireworks have all been the cause of damaging fires. On Catalina, there have been over two hundred human-caused fires in the last one hundred years or so (and only six natural fires). This number and frequency can be devastating to the native ecosystem, causing the disappearance of many species and their eventual replacement with annual grasses and non-native, fire-loving species. Nearly 25 percent of the island has been affected by accidental fires, and recovery depends on the swift and effective actions to help the native ecosystem.

The big 2007 fire, one of Catalina's most epic, was caused by the improper use of a torch by a contractor and burned approximately 10 percent of the entire island, including a home and a number of businesses. The city of Avalon came extremely close to being burned to the ground, and this fire will likely go down in history as the largest and most expensive fire event in the history of the island. Recovery efforts are still ongoing and are expected to continue for years to come.

STEMMING HUMAN-DRIVEN EROSION

Erosion is a natural process on the island. The geological processes that created the island pushed masses of rocks above the sea level, creating its foundation. Once exposed, the elements and other natural processes reverse the process, moving soil and rocks back to the ocean. This is a natural, eternal cycle of construction and deconstruction. The issue we're focusing on is human-driven erosion. Similar to man-made fires, the process of erosion can get out of hand and devastate natural ecosystems.

With no plants to hold it together, soils slumped and eroded after the 2007 fire. The area has since been stabilized. *Courtesy of Catalina Island Conservancy.*

Activities on the landscape that can accelerate the natural processes of erosion include road building and maintenance, urbanization, mining, excessive grazing, intensive agriculture and fire. Many of these human activities are no longer carried out on the island (like cattle-raising and mineral mining), but some, like fire, are likely to be with us for the foreseeable future.

The good news is that man-made erosion is preventable. Employing what are called "Best Management Practices" can reduce or eliminate erosion. Road maintenance can be performed in a way that avoids the accumulation of loose soil that can be carried out to the rivers and, eventually, the ocean. Unnecessary roads can be closed and stabilized through reforestation and replanting of native species, and erosion, when caught early, can be kept in check with plant restoration projects.

Healthy landscapes attract visitors. Ecological balance provides a win-win model for Catalina. *Courtesy of Carlos de la Rosa.*

To Care for It Means to Manage It: A New System of Values and Nature Conservation

As previously mentioned, what we value today is very different than what our ancestors valued on the island. There was a time when shooting an eagle on Catalina was allowed, but today you could serve jail time for the same act. Catalina has set the course for a future in which most of the island is a protected ecosystem. With every season, the island's ecology heals. And there is an emerging ethic on the island that demonstrates a commitment to a future that considers the needs of the land just as much as human needs. The nature of the island is an irreplaceable resource and one that is increasingly important to the long-term economic success of all islanders. In the end, nature conservation is a human-led endeavor that, when accomplished, leads to a mutual benefit.

Chapter 12
REDISCOVERING CATALINA'S RICHES

THE NEW AGE OF DISCOVERY: MODERN RESEARCHERS, NEW SPECIES, OLD SPECIES, GREAT SPECIES!

You would think that with all of the years of biologists, botanists, zoologists and naturalists visiting Catalina, there would be nothing new under the island sun to be discovered—and you would be very wrong. Catalina is full of natural surprises. Every year, several new species are discovered, some of them completely new to science. Catalina has a number of endemic species found nowhere else in the world. The list tops sixty already, and quite a few more are waiting to be discovered. There are a number of species that carry the word *catalinae* as part of their scientific name, including the Catalina Island manzanita (*Arctostaphylos catalinae*), the Catalina Island fox (*Urocyon littoralis catalinae*), the Catalina mariposa lily (*Calochortus catalinae*), the marine clown nudibranch (*Triopha catalinae*), a Turridae seashell (*Antiplanes catalinae*), a tiny endemic longhorn beetle (*Ipochus catalinae*), the Santa Catalina Island bush mallow (*Malacothamnus fasciculatus var. catalinensis*), the Catalina California quail (*Callipepla californica catalinensis*) and a lady beetle that is used in the biological control of whiteflies (*Delphastus catalinae*). And there is another Santa Catalina Island in the Gulf of California near Baja, Mexico, that has several endemic species named *catalinensis*. There is also a species of butterfly with an Avalon-inspired scientific name, the Avalon Hairstreak (*Strymon avalona*).

Above: The Lyon's pygmy daisy, which had not been seen on Catalina since 1931, was rediscovered on the island in 2011. New discoveries like this are one are the outcome of island conservation and exploration. *Courtesy of Tyler Dvorak*.

Left: Former Catalina Island Conservancy botanist Sarah Ratay searches for rare plants. *Courtesy of Catalina Island Conservancy*.

122

New records of plants never before seen on the island also continue to appear thanks to the trained eyes of botanists. Among them, the most spectacular is perhaps the stream orchid (*Epipactis gigantea*), found in a remote canyon on the south side of the island. Also spectacular was the discovery of the tiny endangered Lyon's pygmy daisy (*Pentachaeta lyonii*), not seen on the island since 1931. Both of these species were thought to be extinct on the island until their rediscovery in 2011. The reclassification of the Santa Catalina Island bush mallow as a separate species makes for an extraordinary trio of new findings. There are also a number of species that have already been discovered and are just awaiting proper scientific names!

Prompting these discoveries is a renewed interest in natural history by biologists and researchers combined with the cumulative effects of island-wide restoration efforts by conservancy managers. These new scientists come with both traditional and modern approaches to studying species, from the classic "butterfly net" method to the highly technical DNA analysis. Catalina is slowly revealing new and old secrets as it returns to a more natural state.

ENJOYING WITHOUT DESTROYING: THE RECREATIONAL CONUNDRUM

But Catalina is not just a haven for curious biologists. It is also a longstanding destination for close to a million visitors per year who come to the island for its natural beauty, quaint and relaxed atmosphere, friendly people and numerous cultural and recreational activities. "With close to one million visitors, doesn't this create a huge impact on the island's resources?" you may ask.

Catalina offers its visitors an incredible array of recreational options. Avalon has a variety of excellent hotels and restaurants for every budget and every taste. Cultural activities abound, including music festivals, holiday festivities and parades, historical and cultural tours and access to boating, camping, fishing and hiking. There are activities for every visitor, from the thrilling zip-line ecotours over deep canyons to diving parks, parasailing, glass-bottomed boats and more. The glass-bottomed boat was invented in Avalon, and on a related note, the classic film *The Glass Bottomed Boat*, starring Doris Day, was filmed on Catalina. And, of course, destinations like Two Harbors at the island's isthmus and the conservancy lands also provide endless opportunities for adventure. The island offers many possibilities for nature and outdoor

Avalon is becoming a model ecotourism community. Note the proximity of Avalon to vast natural spaces and the cruise ship in the bay bringing visitors to explore the town and the wilderness. *Courtesy of Frank J. Hein.*

lovers: gorgeous beaches with modest campground facilities, an across-the-island hiking trail (the Trans-Catalina Trail), several annual running events, biking trails, a small private airport with dining facilities and much more. Youth can take advantage of an assortment of summer camps, where they can learn about marine and terrestrial life, camping and outdoor activities.

But all of this activity has to be managed in a way that doesn't damage the protected lands. For example, biking and hiking trails are clearly marked and managed to minimize impacts to the native ecosystems. There are no motorcycles allowed on the interior of the island, and seasonal conservation hunts to reduce numbers of mule deer are carefully managed and controlled by both conservancy personnel and the California Department of Fish and Game—no other hunting is allowed. Camping is restricted to specific campgrounds, where resource use is carefully monitored and managed. Off-trail hiking is discouraged, and no unauthorized collection of plants or animals is allowed.

Recreation is part of the conservancy's mission, and it works to balance this with resource conservation and land management. Its philosophy reflects the belief that protecting a precious natural resource can be done in a way in which people are a part of the equation. It wants visitors to be able to easily access and enjoy protected areas, see conservation in action and learn from it and be part of it. There's no better way to fall in love with the island than to explore it. Breathe in its fresh air, hike its trails, photograph its scenic vistas and feel good about experiencing a place where nature is recovering and, in the process, giving the gift of hope.

Chapter 13
A QUESTION OF BALANCE

Simultaneously managing conservation and tourism in the same location makes for an interesting task. In many ways, conservation of wild areas is seemingly incompatible with inviting thousands of visitors into the very area you're trying to protect. This is the inherent tension that all ecotourism destinations face. Can a sensitive habitat be loved without being loved to death? In some cases, the answer is no. Catalina does have areas to which visitors do not have access. A hidden valley on the island is home to the rarest shrub in North America, the Catalina Island mountain mahogany, where the entire world's population (fewer than a dozen) exist in a single watershed. Making this a touring destination just isn't compatible with the level of protection the species requires to ensure its long-term survival. There are dozens of such sites on Catalina where the risk to the resource requires restrictions to access, but with more than forty-two thousand acres of wilderness to explore, making these areas off limits is non-controversial. But what about the rest of the island? Can it absorb the impact of hundreds of thousands of visitors without losing its ecological integrity? In most cases, the answer is yes, provided access is well planned and carefully executed, but there are some basic guidelines that tour guides and visitors alike need to follow. How does one decide which activities are acceptable in which areas? Getting this right can be something of a balancing act.

A classic example of this balancing act is the relationship between drivers on conservancy lands and wildlife. When cars, roads and wildlife mix, roadkill and near misses are almost certain outcomes. It's bad enough when any animal is hit by a car or bus, but it's a true tragedy if an endangered fox is hit and killed. Although it's certainly possible for most drivers to zip along Catalina's backcountry roads at forty miles per hour, it's not allowed. The maximum speed limit for vehicles on Catalina is twenty-five miles per hour, with no exceptions. A speed this low can be frustrating for drivers who cross Catalina on a regular basis, but that number was chosen to ensure that all drivers are able to brake and avoid wildlife if they dart out onto the road. The speed limit generally makes wildlife lovers happy, but the same can't be said for those who log lots of miles. The important thing from a conservation standpoint is that it keeps foxes alive.

Whatever jobs you've held in your career, odds are that your goal was to make your customers happy. But the work of balancing competing needs while protecting wild places creates a business model in which the main job is not to make everyone happy but to protect the resource. Think of the competing needs of drivers and animals as two ends of a long teeter-totter. Increase the speed limit, and your approval rating among wildlife lovers goes down with the first roadkill, but your approval goes up with drivers. Reduce the speed limit to three miles per hour, and you'll make wildlife lovers very happy but drivers very angry. There's no scenario that will make all parties happy, but there are solutions that make everyone at least content. In this example, a speed limit of twenty-five miles per hour is that solution. There's no shortage of scenarios like this, and there are plenty of hard choices to be made. The key to managing people and resources is education. If everyone truly understands the reason for the speed limit, it becomes much easier to put in place. The same goes for just about any other restriction or requirement that needs to be rolled out. If conservation lies at one end of the teeter-totter and recreation lies at the other, then education is the fulcrum that balances the competing needs and desires.

Thanks in part to residents' inherent love of the island's natural beauty and the trainings and information that have now found their way into this book, Catalina is an example of an ecotourism destination where the community and the conservancy are coming together to deliver high-quality ecotourism adventures while ensuring that Catalina's wild beauty will not just endure but thrive. Islanders pride themselves on the work done toward the protection and restoration of nature just as much as they celebrate the rich human history from which we still learn new lessons every day. We have realized that people are an intrinsic part of the nature of the island—an influential and fundamental component of the conservation effort. Catalina welcomes nearly a million visitors per year, and those wishing to explore the

If you live here, you learn about nature. Conservancy educator Rich Zanelli (right) guides some of Avalon's inquisitive young naturalists. *Courtesy of Alexa Johnson.*

natural beauty that is the hallmark of this place are in the hands of engaged, knowledgeable and enthusiastic guides and residents who make a living at sharing the island's history and ecological wonders.

As a visitor, you too can become part of the island's recovery, as well as let it become part of you. You can take with you the lessons learned here. Apply the knowledge and the experience to your own community. Absorb this philosophy of balance, and make it part of your own life in the places where you live, work and play. In our time here, the island and the people who call it home have taught us more about conservation and community than we could have ever hoped for. We hope this book has somehow conveyed the sense that all things are possible and that nature can be healed if sustained efforts are made.

Catalina is not just a place of recreation. It is a natural laboratory in which we can learn about the past, evaluate the present and plan for the future. It is as much a place for learning as a place for leisure. It is the stage for celebrating great accomplishments, such as the return of nearly lost

Most researchers and biodiversity managers love to share their knowledge with people, especially kids. Pete Dixon from the Catalina Island Conservancy and two of Catalina's emerging naturalists inspect the local flora. *Courtesy of Jack Baldelli.*

species or the discovery of new ones. It is a place where people come to restore their spirits and enjoy unspoiled nature. It is a place to learn about history, geology, archaeology, plants and animals and ourselves. Those of us who have been fortunate enough to live on the island are forever changed by its beauty, complexity, fragility and, ultimately, its resiliency.

PUTTING THE PIECES BACK TOGETHER FOR ALL TO SHARE

Visitors to Catalina Island are often awed by its character. The simple act of traveling to an island in the Pacific is to many a lifelong memory. From the relaxing boat ride to sightings of whales, dolphins, sea lions and seabirds, the crossing of the seemingly bottomless channel (over one mile deep!) really is an adventure all in itself. Once on the island, a world of opportunities and adventures open up to the casual and veteran explorer. Avalon is a quaint, unique community with a rich history, a multicultural background and wonderful people. A day in the water kayaking, exploring the undersea life in semi-subs, snorkeling or diving can be a great place to start. Lunch and dinner are always within walking distance, and live music is bound to be happening on most weekends. A sunrise in Avalon is always a thing of beauty, and only on Catalina would something like a sunrise be unlike other places. You can stand on the shores of western North America, gaze out at the water and watch the sun rise!

But when you visit, be sure to make time for Catalina's natural areas. A day in the interior will get you closer to experiencing California and its rugged coastline as it would have looked thousands of years ago than almost anywhere in the state. And then there are unparalleled views and the chance to encounter giants and dwarves, bison and foxes, quail and eagles. And do keep in mind that some of the best hiking and exploring can be done in the "offseason." During this time, hotels are available, the island is green and the air is cool and fresh. You'll also find a more laid-back atmosphere, perfect for relaxing and recharging.

We hope this book has helped you understand a bit more of what you will encounter on Catalina and that we've challenged you to explore further than you otherwise would have. We hope you'll look for imprints and traces of the past in the broad grassland patches, the old roads and trails and the remnants of structures scattered along the landscape. And we hope that you'll experience and observe the results of the island's ongoing recovery, like the healthy herds of bison, the areas protected and recovering from the epic 2007 fire and the presence of charismatic species like the island fox dashing across the road with agility and speed. Each of these observations represents something unique—a piece of a large puzzle that we have tried to celebrate in this book. When you visit and if you find yourself wondering about anything natural on Catalina, drop by the conservancy's offices and ask; they'll be happy to help you out. If you want to know anything about Avalon or points beyond, just ask a local. They know the island like nobody else and are always happy to help.

Where to from Here?

Through this little book we have explored the many facets of Catalina Island, including the issues and problems that still face us. As island stewards, we continue to learn more and take new approaches to thorny issues. Above all, we seek a balance between conservation and recreation—between experiencing the island's wonders and managing our footprint on the landscape. We produce potable water from the ocean, we recycle extensively and we have implemented island-wide projects to reduce water and electricity consumption. It is already hard to find an incandescent light bulb on the island. Low-flow showerheads are the norm here, and the majority of our toilets flush with salt water, not fresh water. We celebrate the natural world and embrace humanity as we work to make things better. It's hard to imagine all the work ever truly being finished, but we're on a good path and in good company, and it doesn't get much better than that. And here, at the end of your introduction to Wild Catalina Island, we hope that you'll be inspired to walk the paths we walk, hike the hikes we hike and come to love Catalina for the fun and adventure that Avalon and Two Harbors offer but also for its ecological history, its eco-friendly present and its bright and hopeful future. To quote William Wrigley Jr., "In all the world, no trip like this."

FURTHER READING

The following books, articles and websites provide opportunities to delve deeper into some of the topics covered in this book. The list is not intended to be comprehensive but reflects our years of reading through many sources and selecting the best and most accurate.

Adams, Douglas, and Mark Carwardine. *Last Chance to See*. New York: Ballantine Books, 1992.

Coates, Carole. *Catalina Island Pottery and Tile: 1927–1937*. Atglen, PA: Schiffer Publishing, Ltd., 2012.

Coonan, Timothy J., Catherin A. Schwemm and David K Garcelon. *Decline and Recovery of the Island Fox: A Case Study for Population Recovery: Ecology, Biodiversity and Conservation*. Cambridge, England: Cambridge University Press, 2010.

Harden, Deborah. *California Geology*. Upper Saddle River, NJ: Prentice Hall, 2003.

Hogue, Charles L. *Insects of the Los Angeles Basin*. Natural History Museum of Los Angeles County, 1993.

Knapp, Denise A., ed. *Oak Ecosystem Restoration on Santa Catalina Island, California: Proceedings of an on-Island Workshop, February 2–4, 2007*. Catalina Island Conservancy: CreateSpace Independent Publishing Platform, 2011.

Martin, Terrence D., and Jeff Gnass. *Santa Catalina Island: The Story Behind the Scenery*. Wickenburg, AZ: KC Publications, 1984.

McCawley, William. *The First Angelinos: The Gabrielino Indians of Los Angeles*. Banning, CA: Ballena Press, 1996.

Pedersen, Jeannine. *Images of America: Catalina Island*. Charleston, SC: Arcadia Publishing, 2004.

Quammen, David. *The Song of the Dodo: Island Biogeography in an Age of Extinction*. New York: Scribner Publishing, 2011.

White, William Sanford, and Kim Lianne Stotts. *The Wrigley Family: A Legacy of Leadership in Santa Catalina Island*. Glendora, CA: White Limited Editions, 2005.

White, William Sanford, and Steven Kern Tice. *Santa Catalina Island: Its Magic, People and History*. Glendora, CA: White Limited Editions, 2000.

Wicklund, Bruce. *Boat, Dive and Fish Catalina Island*. Avalon, CA: Black Dolphin Diving, 2005.

WEBSITES

Catalina Island Chamber of Commerce and Visitors Bureau. http://www.catalinachamber.com/.

Catalina Island Conservancy. http://www.catalinaconservancy.org/.

Catalina Island Museum. http://www.catalinamuseum.org/.

The Institute for Wildlife Studies (with Catalina eaglecams!) http://www.iws.org/.

INDEX

ABOUT THE AUTHORS

In his life as a naturalist and educator, Frank Hein has served as the director of education for the Catalina Island Conservancy, a bald eagle trapper and tracker, a nature exhibit designer, a bison biologist and a fisheries biologist working on endangered Chinook salmon runs in Northern California. He holds bachelor's degrees in wildlife management and biology from the University of Wisconsin-Stevens Point and a master's degree in environmental policy and management from the University of Denver. Prior to joining the conservancy in early 2010, he served as the president of the Environmental Education Association of Washington and as program manager at the Woodland Park Zoo in Seattle, Washington.

Hein's background in education, communication and ecological investigations led him to develop experiences and programs that now connect over 500,000 people per year to the wonders and values of the natural world. His innovative approach and capacity to connect people to the natural world have earned him statewide, national and international recognition for his efforts. *Wild Catalina Island* emerged from years of research and hands-on experience working with the highly dedicated staff and field personnel of the Catalina Island Conservancy, including co-author Dr. Carlos de la Rosa, an accomplished ecologist and a pretty good guitar player to boot.

A native of Venezuela, Carlos de la Rosa grew up in a big city surrounded by nature, hiking and camping in Ávila National Park, horseback riding on his father's ranch and fishing and boating in the Caribbean Sea. As a biologist, he specialized in aquatic insects and their freshwater ecosystems

Carlos de la Rosa (left) and Frank Hein.

and was published in both scientific and layman's literature. He holds a PhD in ecology from the University of Pittsburgh and has held a number of positions, including scientist, director of biological field stations, director of conservation and education programs and other high-level nonprofit and education positions. He was a biodiversity advisor for the Organization of American States' San Juan River Basin Project in Costa Rica and Nicaragua and served as the environmental management director for the United States Agency for International Development's Northern Zone Consolidation Project in Costa Rica. He was chief conservation and science officer for the Catalina Island Conservancy for six and a half years.

In his current position as director of the La Selva Biological Station operated by the Organization for Tropical Studies in Costa Rica, he oversees one of the most scientifically productive field stations in the tropics, where he puts to full use his multicultural background and experience, scientific knowledge, love for education and sustainability and never-ending sense of wonder about the natural world. As a writer and photographer, he has published several books, a natural history magazine, field guides and posters and has exhibited his photographs in a number of galleries and museums. Together with his co-author Frank Hein, an accomplished naturalist and a pretty good guitar player himself, he spent many evenings in Catalina surrounded by nature and music.